P9-DEX-937

BASEBALL'S *Best Players* RECALL LIFE

Minor MOMENTS

Major MEMORIES

IN THE MINOR LEAGUES

BASEBALL'S *Best Players* RECALL LIFE

Minor MOMENTS
Major MEMORIES

IN THE MINOR LEAGUES

MARK LEINWEAVER

with RYAN BRADLEY

THE LYONS PRESS

Guilford, Connecticut

An imprint of The Globe Pequot Press

The Lyons Press is an imprint of The Globe Pequot Press.

10 9 8 7 6 5 4 3 2 1

Printed in the United States of America

Book design and composition by Diane Gleba Hall

Library of Congress Cataloging-in-Publication Data

Leinweaver, Mark.
   Minor moments, major memories : baseball's best players recall life in the minor leagues
/ Mark Leinweaver.
p.   cm.
   Includes index.
   ISBN 1–59228–735–2 (trade cloth)
1. Minor league baseball—Anecdotes. 2. Baseball players—United States—Anecdotes. I. Title.
GV875.A1L45 2005
796.357'092'2—dc22

                                        2004027843

TO MY WIFE, SARA,
whom I fell in love with
in the Minor Leagues

&

TO MY MOM AND DAD,
who introduced me to
the great game of baseball

Acknowledgments

THIS BOOK was the direct result of the support, energy and hard work of a great number of people, especially my collaborators, Ryan Bradley and J.D. Arteaga. Without them, this project would not have been possible.

In addition, I offer my most sincere thanks to the individuals who helped make this unique idea become a published reality. Thank you Bob Diforio; Tom McCarthy and Lyons Press; Roger LaFrancois; Pete Walker; Luis Sojo; Jason Zillo; Rick Cerrone; Ethan Wilson; Ken Davidoff; Charles Flowers; Peter Chase; Meghan McClure; Mark Teirstein; Steve Nalbandian; Sweeny Murti; Rob Bressler; Brett Quintyne; Farley Chase; Jim Cypher; Jake Jacobson; Scott Hayes; Dave Montgomery; Ira Joe Fisher; Susan Webner; Brian Mahoney; Rick Murphy; Kristina Bradley; the media relations departments of the New York Yankees, New York Mets, Tampa Bay Devil Rays, Toronto Blue Jays, Arizona Diamondbacks, San Francisco Giants, and Boston Red Sox; Paul and Jacki Jakubielski; Matt and Gabrielle Leinweaver; Diane Leinweaver; Dermot Cassidy; Chris Wax; Patti Nannariello; Dan Lafond; Doug Stevens; Kyle Theriault; Matt Ramah; Joe Consigli; Rexy and Maggie.

Introduction

MINOR LEAGUE baseball has been around for more than one hundred years. In small farm towns, bustling blue-collar cities, and everywhere in between across the United States, Canada, and Mexico, almost every Major League Baseball player, manager, and coach has spent time in the minors before making it to the big leagues.

From Portland, Maine, to Portland, Oregon, and Edmonton, Canada, to Monterrey, Mexico, Minor League baseball cities have been the home to some of the greatest stories in the history of the American Pastime. Whether it was on the field, on the bus, or on the side, these dramatic, disappointing, embarrassing, funny, unique, and just plain unusual stories actually happened.

Minor League baseball is also the foundation of a "professional" career for many players, managers, and coaches. It's where the journey all begins, before the big salaries and big time of the big leagues. As a result, the most memorable baseball moments of their lives may have occurred while playing, managing, or coaching in the Minor Leagues.

This book is a collection of memorable Minor League experiences over the past sixty years that take fans into the stands, onto the buses, and into the clubhouses. It highlights a time when these individuals lived together, ate together, traveled together, and played ball together. An era when seventeen-hour bus rides were the norm, forcing the mind to imagine what a two-hour charter flight might be like. A period when the rules of the game were the same, but the stadium lights were dimmer, the crowds were smaller, and the mascot coached first base.

These true stories are the actual accounts as told by the individuals, who range from Major League All-Stars to Minor League journeymen.

Minor League baseball stretches across North America and is played by young men who hail from all over the world. As a result, these individuals are afforded the opportunity to extensively travel and see parts of the continent that they would not have seen otherwise. It gives them a chance to become explorers of sorts.

It puts part-time surfers from southern California in the Great Plains of the Midwest, sons of Texas cattle ranchers in the chilly spring of upper New England and New York City kids in the thick forests of the Pacific Northwest.

Pretend for a moment that you are a Minor League baseball player.

You have just arrived to a city far away from home that you have never even heard of. You rent an apartment, check out the town, and head to the ballpark to work out. You are finally starting to feel as if you are settling into your new environment when it's time to hit the pavement for a road trip.

It's probably fair to say that we have all been on a road trip at some point in our life, whether it was across the state or across the country. Most of us travel by automobile and are used to simple amenities like going at our own pace, tuning the radio, quick rest stops, or even lowering the window for some fresh air.

As bad as a ten-hour trip from New York to Ohio may be by car, even with the family dog sitting between you and your sister, it's far worse on a Minor League bus.

On the bus, you are traveling with thirty other men that will belch, pass gas, play loud music, play live music, keep the light on above their seat after midnight, eat tuna fish sandwiches, and talk to you while you're trying to sleep.

They will even put shaving cream in your palm if you are sleeping and tickle the end of your nose with a pillow, hoping that you will smack your hand against your face in a sub-conscious state of mind.

Not to mention, the bus is probably only traveling between 55 to 60 miles per hour. The air conditioning, when it's work-ing, is either not cold at all or freezing like a meat locker. And if that's not bad enough, you always have to sleep with one eye open just in case the team prankster is zoning in on you as his next victim.

From elementary school physical education classes to Major League Baseball clubhouses, practical jokes, pranks, and stunts are played every single day.

Professional baseball is a business, and as in every business, there are elements that can be very serious. But, unlike in the "real world," baseball involves thousands of grown men play-ing a child's game. As a result, many of these men act like little boys and follow suit with silly, creative, and, occasionally, taste-less behavior.

Baseball is also a numbers game. Minor League baseball sep-arates itself from Major League Baseball through numbers. First, there are many more Minor League players and teams than in the Major League, which simply increases the probabil-ity for this type of conduct. Second, most guys in the minors are single, constantly together, and frankly, quite immature. Depending upon what someone finds humorous, this can be a recipe for disaster.

But, in the end, little boys and girls all over the world dream about making it to the Major Leagues. Even grown men and women, long after their playing days are over, wish they had a chance to strike out a batter or hit a home run in the big leagues.

How many of us would quickly trade places to be in front of a packed house with the game on the line? I would say millions. Well, those millions include Minor Leaguers.

Fortunately for many of the individuals included in this book, they had the opportunity to be in that position. However, those circumstances did not happen by pure chance. It was through hard work, sacrifice, determination, and perhaps a little bit of luck in the Minor Leagues that those people advanced onto the majors.

The idea of this book is to share the exceptionally good and bad unforgettable memories of those that lived the Minor League experience while playing, managing, and coaching in small farm towns, bustling blue-collar cities, and everywhere in between.

Enjoy!

BASEBALL'S *Best Players* RECALL LIFE

Minor MOMENTS

Major MEMORIES

IN THE MINOR LEAGUES

Cal Ripken, Jr.

Major League Clubs / Minor League
Organizations: BALTIMORE ORIOLES

Position: SHORTSTOP, THIRD BASE

Team: ROCHESTER, NY

League: INTERNATIONAL

Year: 1981

CAL RIPKEN is baseball's iron man and
will be a first-ballot Hall of Famer in Cooperstown. His storied twenty-year Major
League career included playing in 2,632 consecutive games, being selected
to the American League All-Star Team nineteen times, hitting 403 home
runs, collecting 1,602 RBI, winning two American League MVP and two
All-Star Game MVP Awards, earning two Gold Gloves, capturing the
1982 AL Rookie of the Year, and winning a World Series title in 1983. On
September 6, 1995, he eclipsed Hall of Fame first baseman Lou Gehrig's
consecutive-games-played streak of 2,130, and even hit a home run on the
record-breaking night.

Ripken played parts of four seasons in the Minor Leagues from 1978
to 1981. His memorable Minor League experience occurred while playing Class AAA ball in the Baltimore Orioles organization.

Author's Note: On April 18, 1981, the Rochester Red Wings of the Baltimore
Orioles organization and the Pawtucket Red Sox of the Boston Red Sox organization played the longest game in professional baseball history. The game lasted
more than eight hours and was stopped at 4:07 A.M. with the scored tied 2–2 after
thirty-two innings. It was completed on June 23, 1981, and won by the Red Sox
3–2 in the bottom of the thirty-third inning at Pawtucket's McCoy Stadium. Cal
Ripken, Jr. was the third baseman for Rochester the entire game.

I laugh when I think about it because we didn't really know any
better about playing that late into the night.

We just kind of played. It was cold and the wind was blowing in really hard. It seemed like a normal, early-season game
with the bad weather, and you would just try to endure and get
through it.

I remember that we were winning 1–0 going into the last inning when there was a triple hit off of the fence. Russ Laribee hit a sac fly and tied the game up 1–1, which sent us to extra innings. I think Russ stayed in the game and struck out his next seven times.

But we just continued to play. We all kind of looked at each other after it got to a certain point, probably about fourteen or fifteen innings, before it seemed like a really long game and just became really bizarre.

Sam Bowen, who was kind of a lifelong Minor Leaguer, was a small, little guy with a compact swing and hit a lot of Minor League home runs. He was considered a bit of a Triple-A superstar in a way and our version of a veteran.

The wind was blowing in so hard that he took a 3–0 pitch, banged it as much as he could hit it and everyone thought that it was out of the ballpark. The game would have been over and it would have been a walk-off homer. The wind brought it back and the outfielder caught it at the fence.

Well, he ran by our dugout and said, "Boys, if that didn't go out, we are going to be here for a long time." I don't remember what inning that was in, but it was kind of like a preface of what was going to be.

People that came out of the game had gone in [the clubhouse], fallen asleep, woke up, and the game was still going on. It was so cold that we were building fires in the dugout. As we went on, we tried to find more available things to burn. I think that we actually burned a couple of broken bats, and people broke some things off the bench. Anything to keep the fire going to stay warm.

I remember that the pitchers were just dominating because the weather was at their advantage. The wind was blowing in and they were very confident. People were throwing goose eggs up on the board, in the form of what would be equivalent to a shutout. There were like nine-inning sections that pitchers were actually pitching. It was just bizarre and weird.

It wasn't until 4:07 A.M. that it was stopped. I think they got some sort of clarification or ruling on the curfew. No one knew for sure what that was all about. The funny part about it was the game ended in a tie, with no conclusion, and we had a day game the very next day.

So, we went back only to have breakfast at an open all-night place and catch a couple hours of sleep. Then, we were back at the ballpark again before noon the next day to start the next game.

Derek Lowe

Major League Clubs/Minor League Organizations:
SEATTLE MARINERS, BOSTON RED SOX

Position: PITCHER

Team: JACKSONVILLE, FL

League: SOUTHERN

Year: 1994

DEREK LOWE won the biggest game in Boston Red Sox history, twice. His dominating performances over the St. Louis Cardinals to clinch the 2004 World Series title and the New York Yankees to capture the American League Championship Series have made him a legend in Beantown. In game 4 of the World Series, Lowe fired seven innings of three-hit shutout baseball to complete a sweep and crown the Red Sox champions for the first time since 1918. Against New York in game 7 of the ALCS, he silenced the Yankees by allowing one run on one hit over six innings to cap the most incredible comeback in the history of professional baseball. As both a closer and starter for the Red Sox, the two-time All-Star recorded 42 saves in 2000 and won 21 games in 2002.

Lowe played parts of seven seasons in the Minor Leagues from 1991 to 1997. His memorable Minor League experience occurred while playing Class AA ball in the Seattle Mariners organization.

I was in Jacksonville, Florida, in 1994, and was at a crossroad. I had about a .500 record in July and I needed to come up with another pitch. I would throw a sinker every once in a while, and in Jacksonville, we had an all-grass infield.

So, ground balls would be great to have there. My pitching coach at the time, Jeff Andrews, told me that every time I throw a fastball to throw a two-seam fastball.

That night, I went out and pitched eight innings and got like twenty ground ball outs. A light clicked off in my head and I knew that I found a pitch. I ran with it and from then on out, I steadily got better. Who knows where I would be if I didn't develop that pitch?

Here we are in 2004, and that was in 1994. If it weren't for that day and learning the sinker, I would not be playing this game right now.

Paul LoDuca

Major League Clubs/Minor League Organizations: LOS ANGELES DODGERS, FLORIDA MARLINS

Position: CATCHER

Team: ALBUQUERQUE, NM

League: PACIFIC COAST

Year: 2000

PAUL LODUCA has established himself as one of the top catchers in baseball. In 2001, he posted a breakout year by batting .320 with 25 home runs and 90 RBI. The two-time All-Star has a career batting average of .285, but many consider him to be one of the better defensive catchers in the National League.

LoDuca played parts of eight seasons in the Minor Leagues from 1993 to 2000. His memorable Minor League experience occurred while playing Class AAA ball in the Los Angeles Dodgers organization.

It was in 2000 after I got sent down in spring training. I was up in the big leagues in 1999 and did well, but then I broke my hand.

So, I was in Triple-A but I wasn't even playing. I was just about ready to hang 'em up. I was just sick and tired of it.

My wife now, who was my fiancée at the time, didn't even know where second base was and basically didn't really know anything about baseball. She was one of those girls that didn't really care if I played or not. She would say, "If you want to play, play."

But, one night after a game, she said to me, "I don't know anything about baseball, but the way you look out on the field looks like you don't even want to be there. So, you either pack up and leave or you start playing."

From that day on, I told myself that I was going to have fun playing again and get to the point where they would have to notice me. I have taken that approach ever since, and it probably turned around my career.

JT Snow

Major League Clubs/Minor League Organizations:
NEW YORK YANKEES, ANAHEIM ANGELS,
SAN FRANCISCO GIANTS
Position: FIRST BASE
Team: PRINCE WILLIAM, VA
League: CAROLINA
Year: 1990

JT SNOW is one of the greatest defensive first basemen in the past half century. In addition to his seven Gold Gloves and two best defensive first basemen awards, he has produced three 20-plus home run and four 95-plus RBI seasons during his thirteen-year Major League career. In the 2002 World Series, he led San Francisco with a .417 batting average over seven games.

Snow played parts of six seasons in the Minor Leagues from 1989 to 1994. His memorable Minor League experience occurred while playing Class A ball in the New York Yankees organization.

It was my most embarrassing moment in baseball. I was in Single-A with the Yankees in Prince William, Virginia.

I was hitting third that day, and I had been hitting third a lot of the year. The first guy up hit a lead-off home run and the second hitter made an out. Then, I came up and struck out.

Well, there was nobody on base, so I threw my bat and helmet to the dugout, put my head down, and started walking down the first-base line. I heard the crowd snickering and stuff, and I got about two-thirds of the way down the first-base line when I looked up and saw the other team just getting done throwing the ball around the infield.

I looked up at the scoreboard and saw that there were two outs. I said to myself, "Oh, man." I walked off the field and back to the dugout.

We were playing at home and had about one thousand people there that night. They were good fans but they were laughing, cheering and ribbing me, having a good time. For the rest of the game, whether I was playing first and caught a ball or something, they would remind me how many outs there were.

That's the most embarrassing thing, when you forget how many outs there are. I've done it at first base, too, when I'd catch the second out of the inning and think it's the third out. Man, it's embarrassing.

Mike Piazza

Major League Clubs/Minor League
Organizations: NEW YORK METS,
LOS ANGELES DODGERS,
FLORIDA MARLINS

Position: CATCHER

Team: BAKERSFIELD, CA

League: CALIFORNIA

Year: 1991

MIKE PIAZZA is the greatest offensive
catcher of all time. The eleven-time All-
Star has hit more than 350 home runs and is the all-time leader in home
runs by a catcher, breaking Hall of Famer Carlton Fisk's record of 351 on
May 5, 2004. He has also collected more than 1,100 RBI, has a lifetime .315
batting average, and hit more than 30 home runs in a season eight times
in his career.

Piazza played parts of four seasons in the Minor Leagues from 1989
to 1992. His memorable Minor League experience occurred while playing
Class A ball in the Los Angeles Dodgers organization.

The Minor Leagues were not so much about one game or
home runs. To me, it was the innocence of it. The camaraderie of the guys, the fact that you're not making a ton of money,
that you all have the same dream and you're driven by that
dream.

In some ways, it was just as, if not more enjoyable, than the
big leagues. Don't get me wrong, obviously up here is where you
want to be. But down there, there was nothing but the game and
that sort of common thread that ties you together.

It was fun and we had fun. I was fortunate because I came
up through the Dodgers organization and their emphasis was
on the Minor Leagues. We had five Rookies of the Year in a row.
They had quality players but they also drafted fun guys, good

guys. From my first experience in instructional league to my last year in Triple-A, I had a lot of fun.

I remember one time we were in Modesto, California, and staying in a hotel with no money for a car or a cab. The only thing open for food after the game was a Taco Bell drive through. We were starving because we had a bus ride and long game that day.

The two kids working at the drive through window would not serve us because we walked up and didn't have a car. We were asking people driving by if they could order us some stuff. But, we soon figured that we didn't want those people to run off with our money or food.

So Greg Hansell, who was my Minor League roommate, got up on my back and went to the drive through. When they said, "Can we help you?" I started making car noises like, "Ruhn, ruhn, ruhn, ruhn" while he said, "I would like two soft chicken tacos, a bean burrito . . ." and so on.

We went around the front while I'm going, "Beep, beep" with him on my back like he was in a car. Finally, the manager just broke down and said that they would serve us because we were just so desperate for food.

There were also these two guys who I played with in the Minor Leagues that were just so cheap. Minor League meal money was about $9 per day in A ball. They saved their $9 by going to the supermarket and getting a loaf of bread, peanut butter, and jelly. They would make peanut butter and jelly sandwiches the whole road trip, if you could believe that.

I was astounded! I couldn't wait for my dad to come visit me because I knew that he would give me a couple of hundred dollars for the effort. To me, that was a goldmine. I would take all of my roommates out to dinner and we would just splurge.

Families were also big. When someone's dad or mom came, that was fair game because they had to take their son's roommate out for dinner. You got to know places like unlimited salad and breadsticks at The Olive Garden, where you would just gorge yourself on salad and breadsticks so you weren't hungry.

Stuff like that. Stuff like trying to beg the bus driver or your coach to stop for beer so that you could have beer and drink it on the bus ride home.

Robby Hammock

Major League Clubs/Minor League Organizations:
ARIZONA DIAMONDBACKS

Position: CATCHER

Team: LETHBRIDGE, ALBERTA, CANADA

League: PIONEER

Year: 1998

ROBBY HAMMOCK has become an important part of five-time Cy Young Award winner Randy Johnson's impressive Hall of Fame résumé. In just his second big league season, Hammock caught Johnson's perfect game against the Atlanta Braves on May 18, 2004. He was also behind the plate for The Big Unit's 4,000th career strikeout on June 29 versus the San Diego Padres. In his rookie year, he batted .282 with eight home runs and 28 RBI in 65 games played.

Hammock played parts of five seasons in the Minor Leagues from 1998 to 2002. His memorable Minor League experience occurred while playing Class A ball in the Arizona Diamondbacks organization.

When I first signed in 1998, I had just come out of the University of Georgia where you played three or four days a week.

I went right into pro ball after signing as a catcher. I was a later round draft pick and not playing at first. The first week-and-a-half to two weeks, I didn't even sniff the field.

Then, a guy got hurt and another catcher moved up, so I started catching every day. I mean *every* day. Sixteen days in a row, then an off-day, and then ten days in a row.

In the Pioneer League, the bus rides were nine- to thirteen-hour bus rides. We would take batting practice and infield every day, every day. I didn't know any better. I just thought it was how it went. I didn't know to change clothes after batting practice and infield. I wore the same thing as soon as I got there.

Being a catcher, I would even catch bullpens every day before batting practice. I would get there and suit up in full uniform with jock strap and a cup. We never wore shorts. After bullpens, we would go right into stretch, take batting practice, infield, and then I'd catch the game.

I played 66 games in about sixty-nine days and was just trying to get by each day. I didn't know if I was cut out to do this. It was terrible. I never changed and wore the same black cotton undershirt that turned brown by the end of the season.

I now look back on it and laugh.

Junior Spivey

Major League Clubs/
Minor League Organizations:
ARIZONA DIAMONDBACKS,
MILWAUKEE BREWERS

Position: SHORTSTOP

Team: HIGH DESERT, CA

League: CALIFORNIA

Year: 1997

JUNIOR SPIVEY broke out in 2002 as one of the best second basemen in the National League. Prior to the 2004 season, Spivey was part of a blockbuster trade that sent him to the Milwaukee Brewers with Craig Counsell, Lyle Overbay, Chad Moeller, Chris Capuano, and Jorge de la Rosa for slugger Richie Sexson. The All-Star middle infielder had his best season in '02, batting .301 with 16 home runs, 78 RBI, six triples, and 11 stolen bases.

Spivey played parts of six seasons in the Minor Leagues from 1996 to 2001. His memorable Minor League experience occurred while playing Class A ball in the Arizona Diamondbacks organization.

We were playing in Visalia in 1997 and it was my first full season of pro ball.

There was a really nice-looking girl in the stands. She was staring at me and I was checking her out. After an out, I ran onto the field and blew her a kiss.

Well, I got banged for that in Kangaroo Court. They busted me and I had to pay a fine. They ran with it, putting a lot of pressure on me and talking about how I was going to get released for doing something like that.

They gave me a hard time, but it was all fun and games. We had a great time with it.

Mike Mussina

Major League Clubs/Minor League Organizations:
BALTIMORE ORIOLES, NEW YORK YANKEES

Position: PITCHER

Team: HAGERSTOWN, MD

League: EASTERN

Year: 1990

MIKE MUSSINA has been one baseball's most dominating pitchers since the early 1990s. The five-time All-Star has collected 211 wins, recorded 2,258 strikeouts, and complied 2,833 innings through his fourteen-year career. He has also won 15 or more games nine times. Recognized as an incredibly durable pitcher, Mussina has tossed at least 200 innings in a season ten times and has won six Gold Glove Awards.

Mussina played parts of two seasons in the Minor Leagues from 1990 to 1991. His memorable Minor League experience occurred while playing Class AA ball in the Baltimore Orioles organization.

I t was my first week of pro ball and I was in Hagerstown, Maryland, in July of 1990. I reported right after July 4th. We played about a weeklong home stand and then were getting ready to go on a road trip.

This was my first bus trip as a professional. I brought my stuff to the field, left it in my car, and after the game, got it out and brought it by the clubhouse.

The bus driver pulled up to the clubhouse and opened the bay to put our stuff under the bus. Three or four of us put our suitcases down right next to the bay. We then walked over to get on the bus when suddenly the driver moved it.

As the bus started moving, I said to myself, "Wait a minute, what's going on?" I turned and looked over my shoulder just in time to see him run over the three or four bags sitting by the back tire compartment. He ran over the bags, including mine, with an I-don't-know-how-many-ton bus!

So, there was my suitcase, which was supposed to be square or rectangular, just mashed. The bag was destroyed. I almost couldn't unzip it to get it open. There were shoes propped upright that had the soles snapped in half. I had a belt in there that the buckle just compressed together.

We hadn't even left on the road yet, in fact I hadn't even been on the road ever, and the bus driver ran over my bags sitting next to the back wheel.

It was one of those things that you'd say, "Hey, hey, hey!" when it was happening and then it was too late. I had no choice but to still put the bag on the bus and take it on the trip.

A few weeks later, we were in London, Ontario, Canada, which was the Detroit Tigers Double-A team in the Eastern League at the time.

We played a game, don't remember if we won or lost, and went out to the bus. It was not a get-away day but the hotel was not right around the corner, either.

We all got on the bus, the driver fired it up, and then the bus started smoking. The driver told us, "Get off the bus, get off the bus, get off the bus!"

The bus caught on fire.

We got off the bus and were standing around for a little while when the driver said, "We're done. The bus isn't running."

I remember standing out there thinking, "Now what?"

Getting cabs was going to be hard to do, so we decided to grab our stuff and start walking from the stadium to the hotel carrying equipment, bags, and other baseball stuff. There weren't as many bags as there were people, so we would walk about ten minutes and then trade off with someone else to carry the equipment.

It took us about fifty minutes to an hour to get back. There were our twenty-two guys and coaches, trekking a few miles across town, back to the hotel at night after the game.

Fortunately, I only spent about seven weeks in Double-A.

Those kinds of things are funny after they are over. But, when you get your bag run over, the bus catches on fire, and you have to hike a few miles back to the hotel, it's not exactly how you envision pro ball.

Joe Borowski

Major League Clubs/Minor League
Organizations: CHICAGO CUBS,
BALTIMORE ORIOLES, CHICAGO
WHITE SOX, MILWAUKEE BREWERS,
ATLANTA BRAVES, NEW YORK
YANKEES, CINCINNATI REDS

Position: PITCHER

Team: NEWARK, NJ

League: INDEPENDENT

Year: 2000

JOE BOROWSKI was one of the best stories in baseball in 2003. After fighting to rejoin the Major League ranks the season before, he emerged as one of the National League's premier closers when he saved 33 games for the Chicago Cubs. A former journeyman with stops in Baltimore, Atlanta, and New York since 1995, Joe had saved a total of two games before his breakout season with Chicago in '03.

Borowski played parts of twelve seasons in the Minor Leagues from 1990 to 2001. His memorable Minor League experience occurred while playing independent ball in a non-affiliated organization.

After 1998 with the Yankees, I signed as a free agent with Milwaukee in 1999. I got hurt in the spring and wound up pitching the whole year hurt. I had a garbage year.

I signed with Cincinnati that off-season with promises of them needing me and that there were two spots open in the big leagues. So, I went to spring training and there were like forty-eight pitchers in camp. After one day of big league games, which I didn't even get to pitch in, I got sent down.

I went down to minor-league camp and after about a week and a half, I hadn't even thrown in a game. I knew that I wasn't going to be there very long, and sure enough, about five days before camp broke, I got released.

All of the teams that I was going to sign with that off-season were all trying to get rid of guys. I had nowhere to go and wound up going home. I sat at home for a month, did nothing, and ended up going to independent ball because there was a team ten minutes from my house. Talk about miserable. It was the worst experience of my life. It was like playing American Legion ball.

You play because you love the game. Well, I started to resent it. I didn't care whether I did good or bad, or if I was late to the field. It just didn't matter to me anymore.

I called my wife, and this was around July 5, and told her that at the end of the month I was going to retire if I didn't sign with another team. Now, I don't know if I would have done that or not. I don't know.

Maybe two days later, a friend of mine named Danny Rios got a job in Mexico. At the time, I was getting paid about $2,400 per month. I got an offer to play in Mexico for about $9,000 per month and thought that anything had to be better than this. He gave me the name of a guy from down there and I called the guy that night. The next day, he called back and said that there were three teams that would sign me right away.

I ended up signing with Monterrey on July 10. It didn't matter down there about what round you were in or how much money you were getting. You either did good or you went home. I really started to enjoy the game again.

While I was playing, I saw an old coach of mine from the Orioles that was now in charge of scouting for Latin America with the Cubs. He saw me pitch and the next day said that the Cubs would sign me for the rest of the year. I told him that I didn't want to burn any bridges down here, and that if he wanted to sign me for next year, I would be more than willing.

That off-season, they signed me and I played in Triple-A in 2001 with the Cubs. I got a break in 2002 out of spring training and made the team. I lucked out, caught a few breaks, and have been able to put together a couple of good years.

Roy Halladay

Major League Clubs/Minor League Organizations: TORONTO BLUE JAYS
Position: PITCHER
Team: DUNEDIN, FL
League: GULF COAST LEAGUE
Year: 1995

ROY HALLADAY won the American League Cy Young Award in 2003 after posting a 22–7 record with a 3.25 ERA. He set career highs in strikeouts with 204 and innings pitched with 266. The two-time All-Star, who won 19 games in 2002, has compiled a 67–39 record with a solid 3.89 ERA and 702 strikeouts in seven big league seasons.

Halladay played parts of six seasons in the Minor Leagues from 1995 to 2001. His memorable Minor League experience occurred while playing Class A ball in the Toronto Blue Jays organization.

When I first signed out of high school in 1995, I got drafted in June and ended up signing on July 1.

I got a call after the contract was done and told that I was leaving tomorrow. So, I went home and hurried everything together in a bag to go to Dunedin, Florida, from Colorado. It all happened so fast that I had little idea of what I was supposed to be doing.

They told me that I was going to play in the Gulf Coast League and that there would be an airport limo to pick me up. That was first time that I had been away on my own. I was thinking that a big, black stretch limo was going to pick me up and drive me home.

When I got to the airport after landing in Dunedin, I went outside and there was no such thing. I started calling people from back home, trying to figure out what I was supposed to do. I came to find out that the airport limo was one of those vans that picked up like fifteen people and dropped them off home by home. Because I missed that one, they sent out a clubhouse guy to pick me up.

We started heading back to the field when he said that he had to make one quick stop. He pulled into the county jail and had to pick up one of their clubhouse guys, who got thrown in jail the previous night. We went to the penitentiary and bailed the guy out. He hopped in and they brought me to this Countryside Inn on a Friday afternoon. They said, "See you Monday morning." I had never been away by myself.

That is when it sunk in. I had no idea. I thought that I was going to go and meet Cito Gaston, Joe Carter, and spend a little time in Dunedin before I went up and played with them. It was amazing how oblivious I was to what I was in for. That was the biggest shocker for me, and right from then, I knew what was going on.

That weekend I panicked. I had no idea as to where I was supposed to go. Fortunately, maybe a block down the street, there was a mall. I walked over to the mall, got something to eat and goofed around there for the weekend. I found out that on Monday, the van came over and picked us up to take us to the field. There were also a few more guys staying there that I didn't even meet until Monday.

I grew up in a blue-collar area that did not have a big diversity of people. I think in my high school, there may have been one black student there. All of a sudden, I go over to the field where there were Latin guys speaking Spanish and people from all over the world. It was an eye-opener. I had three guys approach me that I ended up being roommates with. We had four guys in an apartment, one Latino guy and two African-American guys.

It was a quick turn from where I came from, and one of those things that you don't see what's outside of where you are from until you get there.

Doug Mientkiewicz

Major League Clubs/Minor League Organizations: MINNESOTA TWINS, BOSTON RED SOX

Position: FIRST BASE

Team: NEW BRITAIN

League: EASTERN

Year: 1998

DOUG MIENTKIEWICZ recorded the most meaningful putout in Boston Red Sox history, catching an underhand toss from Keith Foulke for the final out of the 2004 World Series. Considered to be one of the best defensive first basemen in the American League, he won a Gold Glove Award in 2001 and hit .300 twice in his first five big league seasons. His best year was in 2001, when he batted .306 with 15 home runs and 74 RBI to help lead the Twins to their first winning season in nine years. In July of 2004, he was acquired by Boston in a four-team trade that included Nomar Garciaparra being sent to the Chicago Cubs.

Mientkiewicz played parts of five seasons in the Minor Leagues from 1995 to 2000. His memorable Minor League experience occurred while playing Class AA ball in the Minnesota Twins organization.

Double-A, 1998. It was the last game of the season and we were one game up to go to the playoffs.

The team behind us had already won. It was raining, just pouring. I was leading the league in hitting, and the guy behind me, Michael Barrett, went like 5-for-5 to go two points ahead of me.

I was also one hit away from the New Britain single-season record for hits in a season and the batting title. We were thinking that if we didn't play, we were still a half-game up, and so we would win. Well, the team had some special promotion that night and were expecting a sellout, and they wanted to play.

To us, going to the playoffs meant more than their stupid promotion. So, nine guys went out on the field at about 5:30 P.M. and started pulling the tarp off. Guys were throwing buckets of water on the field.

Then, the owner came down and asked us what the hell we were doing. He just reamed us out.

My manager, John Russell, pulled me aside and told me that we had to go to talk to the general manager. I said, "We? No, you. You're the manager. I don't have to do anything." But I said, "Alright." So, we went up and talked to him.

We ended up playing the game and winning. I went something like 2-for-3.

That year, Russell worked with me from day one. He always told me that I would hit .300 in the big leagues, do it more than once, and have the chance to win a Gold Glove. He was hard on me, but he made me believe that I could accomplish what I did in the big leagues.

That Eastern League team in '98 was pretty good, and that whole group went to the big leagues the next year. That group was pretty close and included Jacque Jones, Torii Hunter, Chad Allen, Christian Guzman, Corey Koskie, and A. J. Pierzynski.

We played together so long that we knew what everybody could do. We were always very supportive of one another, whether it was baseball-oriented, family life, or whatever. We would help each other out with finances, places to live, or little things like borrowing a car to pick up a family member. I was fortunate because whatever I needed, no matter what it was, how ridiculous it was, or how time-consuming it was, I had guys willing to do that for me.

I remember I was making about $1,110 a month then. My first year on the forty-man roster, I cleared $52 every two weeks after paying bills and other stuff. I always found the cheapest dinners and stuff like that.

Everyday in the minors up until that second season in Double-A, I thought that I wouldn't make it to the big leagues. I didn't think that I had enough power or could hit big league pitching. But that was the level when you started to see guys that you played against get a chance in the big leagues. Then, when you got to the big leagues, you started to see the same guys that you played against in Trenton or in Akron.

Aubrey Huff

Major League Clubs/Minor League Organizations:
TAMPA BAY DEVIL RAYS

Position: THIRD BASE, FIRST BASE, OUTFIELD

Team: ORLANDO, FL

League: SOUTHERN

Year: 1999

AUBREY HUFF became the Tampa Bay Devil Rays franchise player in 2003 after setting club records for doubles with 47, home runs with 34, and slugging percentage with a .555 mark. He also posted a .311 average and a career high 107 RBI. In 2004, Huff continued his production with 29 home runs and 105 RBI.

Huff played parts of five seasons in the Minor Leagues from 1998 to 2002. His memorable Minor League experience occurred while playing Class AA ball in the Tampa Bay organization.

It was my Double-A year in 1999, and we won the Southern League Championship. It came down to the final game of the regular season. We just played and won in Huntsville, Alabama, and were waiting to see if Jacksonville won or not.

If they won, we go home because our season is over with. But Jacksonville ended up losing, and so we had to travel all the way back there to play a one-game playoff to see who would advance to the Division Series.

The Southern League was the worst traveling league in Minor League baseball. Orlando-to-Jacksonville was the shortest trip there was, but from Orlando, we would go to places like Mobile, Alabama, and Jackson, Tennessee.

These were sixteen-, eighteen-hour long bus rides. We would travel all night and wake up the next morning in the city that we were playing in that night. Me and a teammate would be doubled-up on the bus, and the only way we could get to sleep was to get bottle of Captain Morgan's spiced run and drink it.

We had a saying of, "We'll sail with the Captain" to get us through the bus trips and help us get to sleep. The memories . . . waking up with that taste like a cat shit in your mouth. We would try to drink so much that we would just pass out.

In those Minor League seasons, you just wanted to be done at the end of the season. But we were going to play a one-game playoff. I remember it like it was yesterday. We wanted to win, sure, but if we didn't, it wasn't the end of the world.

We had a situation where we were up 1–0 because I hit a home run off a left-handed guy with a nasty slider. I never hit home runs in the Minor Leagues off left-handed sliders. So, out of all the games to do it, it was that one. It was 1–0 through the ninth inning, and during the game, Jacksonville had the bases loaded with nobody out like three times. But each time, they would ground into a double play, and the next guy would pop out or something. We always got out of the jam.

We ended up winning the game 1–0 and went on to win the whole thing. It was an extra two more weeks of the season. But looking back on it, I'm glad we won it because if you're there, you might as well do it.

Mike Lowell

Major League Clubs/Minor League
Organizations: NEW YORK YANKEES,
FLORIDA MARLINS

Position: THIRD BASE

Team: NORWICH, CT

League: EASTERN

Year: 1995

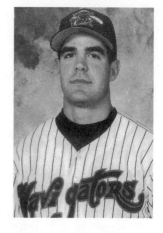

MIKE LOWELL became one of the best
third basemen in the National League seem-
ingly overnight. In 2003, he posted a career year by belting 32 home runs
and collecting 105 RBI while leading the Florida Marlins to a World Series
Championship. After joining the Marlins, the three-time All-Star produced
five straight 85-plus RBI campaigns and averaged 24 home runs per year.

Lowell played parts of five seasons in the Minor Leagues from 1995
to 1999. His memorable Minor League experience occurred while playing Class AA ball in the New York Yankees organization.

I remember playing in Norwich and after the game, we would
go down the road to this lady's restaurant.

We didn't have to pay for food as long as we cooked it. She
would say, "As long as you can cook it, you can eat it."

So, we would pay for a beer and then go into the kitchen to
cook burgers and make sandwiches.

Jason Varitek

Major League Clubs/Minor League Organizations:
SEATTLE MARINERS, BOSTON RED SOX

Position: CATCHER

Team: PORT CITY, NC

League: SOUTHERN

Year: 1995

JASON VARITEK exemplifies preparation, inspiration, and leadership. The heart and soul of the 2004 World Series Champion Boston Red Sox, Varitek guided his team to the most remarkable comeback in Major League baseball history in the American League Championship Series over the New York Yankees by batting .321 with two home runs, seven RBI, and 68 innings caught. The All-Star catcher had a career year in '04, posting a .296 average with 18 home runs and 73 RBI.

Varitek played parts of three seasons in the Minor Leagues from 1995 to 1997. His memorable Minor League experience occurred while playing Class AA ball in the Seattle Mariners organization.

The thing that I appreciated most about the Minor Leagues was the time that a man named Roger Hansen, the catching instructor in Seattle, spent with me. It was a tremendous amount of time that he spent with me.

Basically, he worked and worked and worked with me on different things behind the plate. Finally, they all came to me. He kept encouraging me and would say, "You'll see the light at the end of the tunnel. It will be there. It's not that far away."

I just couldn't get some things right, and do some things. I thank him the most for anything that happened for me in the Minor Leagues.

I struggled a lot in the Minor Leagues. There was a lot of development and I got better by learning how to struggle. My wife was with me through all of the tough times, and that was key for me. After my first year, we got married and she was with me all of the time. She was my own psychologist and my support.

The biggest adjustment for me was going from having to win in college to development. You were not always playing with guys that had the same goals right then, like win that game and win as many games as you can.

You had a lot more selfish play. I think that was the biggest culture shock for me. That was a realization. It took a long time to adjust, and I still never really adjusted to that mentality.

Andy Phillips

Major League Clubs/Minor League
Organizations: NEW YORK YANKEES
Position: INFIELDER
Team: COLUMBUS, OH
League: INTERNATIONAL
Year: 2003

ANDY PHILLIPS is a rising star and top prospect in the New York Yankees organization. In his first Major League at-bat versus the Boston Red Sox at Fenway Park on September 26, 2004, he pinch hit for Alex Rodriguez and homered over the Green Monster. In 2004, he batted a career best .315 with 30 home runs and 101 RBI between Double-A Trenton and Triple-A Columbus and won the Triple-A All-Star Game for the International League with a game-winning home run in the bottom of the tenth inning.

Phillips has played six seasons in the Minor Leagues from 1999 to 2004. His memorable Minor League experience occurred while playing Class AAA ball in the New York Yankees organization.

To be able to end the Triple-A All-Star Game, and end it in the right way with a walk-off homer to win it for the home team, was my most memorable moment of the Minor Leagues.

In the tenth, I thought that there were three guys in front of me. I guess I miscalculated the line-up and soon realized that I was coming up third that inning. The first two guys were quick outs, and the guy pitching had not given up a hit. He got five consecutive outs.

In my first at-bat, I struck out on three pitches. I was basically trying not to embarrass myself. When you're in the on-deck circle, it crosses your mind about ending the game with one swing. You look up and see that there are two outs. I got a 1–0 hanging slider. I can still see the moment, even the pitch. It was pretty cool.

It was a unique deal because there are not too many times that Boston fans will cheer for a Yankees player. To do it in Pawtucket, in that setting with the place packed, the people were going crazy. Everybody was very supportive. It was probably the only time in my career, as long as I'm wearing a Yankee uniform, that Red Sox fans will be supportive of anything that I do.

The first thing that I noticed when the ball crossed the fence was our whole dugout swarming to the plate. That was very cool because here were a bunch of guys that I didn't even really know. With it being an All-Star Game, I knew of these guys, but the next day I was going back to compete against them.

Anytime you go to something like that, in the back of your mind, you want do something special. That was the biggest moment of my career, being the Player of the Game and being interviewed on national TV.

By the time I walked off of the field and got into the clubhouse, I had twenty-three voicemails on my cell phone. Over the next two days, I got about sixty calls or voicemails.

Tim Salmon

Major League Clubs/Minor League Organizations: ANAHEIM ANGELS
Position: OUTFIELD
Team: MIDLAND, TX
League: TEXAS
Year: 1991

TIM SALMON was one of the best power hitters of the 1990s and perhaps the most productive player in baseball to have never been named an
All-Star. In his twelve big league seasons, the 1993 American League
Rookie of the Year has a career batting average of .283 with 290 home
runs and 989 RBI. Salmon's most outstanding season came in 1995, when
he batted .330 with 34 homers and 105 RBI. Two seasons later, he posted
a career-best 129 RBI. In the 2002 postseason against the Yankees, Twins,
and Giants, he helped lead the Angels to the World Series title by batting
.288 with four home runs and 12 RBI.

Salmon played parts of four seasons in the Minor Leagues from 1989
to 1992. His memorable Minor League experience occurred while playing Class AA ball in the Anaheim Angels organization.

The one thing that stood out for me was in Double-A in Midland, Texas.

At that time, whenever you hit a home run, they would pass
around the hat in the stands. It was a nice way to make some extra
cash. In the Minor Leagues, you were not getting paid much.

Fernando Valenzuela, who was with the big club, came
down on a rehab with us in Double-A. Everyone was pumped
up that Fernando was going to be there, but then we heard the
news that the place would be completely sold out.

When we got there for the game, they had the outfield warning track roped off and the stands were full. It was just a packed
house. Guys were saying, "Boy, if you could just hit a home run
today, wouldn't that be awesome. The kind of money you could
bring in."

In the first few innings, everyone was just swinging for the fences. In about the third or fourth inning, I hit a home run. I was pumped running around the bases, thinking, "Oh my gosh, I am going to make a ton of money."

Two batters later, Damien Easley hit a home run. All of a sudden, I'm like, "No way!" They were still passing around my hat, and people were going to put money in for me and for him.

It was a bummer because we ended up having to split the pot. I was thinking that it should have all been my money because I hit the first one. I was the one that got people excited in the first place. I think we got close to $300 a piece.

That story will always stand out for me. One, because of Fernando Valenzuela and as big as he was then. And two, the fact that I hit a home run when I was trying to.

I remember taking my wife out to dinner at an actual sit-down restaurant. Up until then, it was fast food or an all-you-can-eat place most of the time. Things were pretty tight, so hitting those home runs definitely helped ease the pain a little bit.

Rich Gedman

Major League Clubs/Minor League Organizations: BOSTON RED SOX, HOUSTON ASTROS, ST. LOUIS CARDINALS, NEW YORK YANKEES

Position: CATCHER

Team: PAWTUCKET

League: INTERNATIONAL

Year: 1980

RICH GEDMAN played thirteen seasons in the Major Leagues. The two-time All-Star, who helped lead the Red Sox to two postseason appearances in 1986 and '88, posted a career year in 1985 by belting 18 home runs and collecting 80 RBI. Truly faithful Red Sox fans will never forget Gedman's pinch-hit grand slam home run at Tiger Stadium during Boston's drive to the pennant in 1986.

Gedman played parts of six seasons in the Minor Leagues from 1977 to 1982. His memorable Minor League experience occurred while playing Class AAA ball in the Boston Red Sox organization.

We were in Charleston, West Virginia, in 1980, and got rained out for three straight days. We were all cooped up and hardly had any meal money or anything like that. None of us had credit cards and we basically lived off our meal money.

We tried to make ends meet with what we had, so we pooled our money together and bought a few pizzas. If you were one of the guys that played cards and had a little extra where somebody didn't, you helped them find a way to get by. That was what those trips were about, survival in the Minor Leagues.

The guys were basically having pizza and beer, playing cards, and doing whatever we could do to kill time. One thing led to another and all of a sudden, we had ten or twelve guys cooped up in a room coming up with these strange ideas like, "Can you tear a telephone book?" We had pizza boxes all over and beer bottles, too. Basically, over the three days, we ended up trashing the room. I was in Triple-A with Pawtucket and being kids, we didn't even clean it up and just left it for the maids.

When we got back home, we were called into the office before going out to take batting practice. I think everyone got fined fifty dollars apiece to clean up the room with a slap on the hand and told that we represent the club. Everyone understood that and was willing to do what they had to do to take care of the room. Fifty dollars was a lot of money then. It was pretty steep but it also taught us a lesson.

The only reason that I bring it up is because it happened pretty early in the year and I don't remember anything like that happening again. It was a three-day stint in a town where there was very little to do. There was no place to go and baseball was it. Toward the end of the year, we just came back from our New York road trip where we went to Syracuse and Rochester.

The first day in we go out for BP and someone came out on the field and said, "Joe (Morgan) wants to see you." I thought to myself, "Oh my God," trying to rack my brain as to what I did. The only time he called me in the office was when I did something wrong. I said to myself, "What the hell did we do this time?" I couldn't come up with anything but I was a little timid walking into the room. It was almost the identical thing that happened the last time.

I walked in and there were the guys sitting with Joe, who started to go into what happened. He said, "I just want to congratulate all you boys, you are going to be September call-ups." My heart jumped out of my chest! Here I was thinking that I was in trouble. At the time, I was hitting about .230 with maybe 11 home runs and 30 RBI. That was the furthest thing from my mind.

We had about a week left in our season, and I was going to the big leagues. It was that dream come true, knowing that you were going to put on that Red Sox uniform for a month and see what the Major Leagues were like. It's weird how things happen, when that opportunity comes along and you don't know when it's going to be or how.

I always tried to figure out how I deserved it because I thought that I had a terrible second half. That was a very, very special day, but certainly not one that started out that way in my mind.

Cliff Politte

Major League Clubs/Minor League Organizations:
ST. LOUIS CARDINALS, PHILADELPHIA PHILLIES,
TORONTO BLUE JAYS, CHICAGO WHITE SOX

Position: PITCHER

Team: LITTLE ROCK, AR

League: TEXAS

Year: 1997

CLIFF POLITTE broke into the Major Leagues with the St. Louis Cardinals in 1998, one of the most memorable seasons in baseball. Politte has proven to be a very serviceable pitcher, working as a starter, long reliever, set-up man, and closer in his big league career. In 2003, he saved a career-high 12 games for the Toronto Blue Jays.

Politte played parts of five seasons in the Minor Leagues from 1996 to 2000. His memorable Minor League experience occurred while playing Class AA ball in the St. Louis Cardinals organization.

It was the 1997 season, and I was playing in Little Rock, which was the Double-A affiliate of the St. Louis Cardinals. Tom Pagnozzi came down to rehab because I think that he had a bad knee at the time. They wanted him to catch a few games before he went back up.

He caught three of the games that I was starting, and I think that I only gave up two earned runs the whole time that he caught me. I threw something like eight innings the first game, seven the second, and maybe six or seven in the third game. I allowed only six or seven hits over the three games.

I'm from St. Louis, so Tom and I knew some of the same people because he made his home there. We kind of hit it off a little bit. I remember one night we were in Shreveport, Louisiana, and Tom had invited the whole team out after a game. We got clobbered in a two-game series there the week before, and so Tom invited the team to go out with him to have a couple of drinks and take our minds off of baseball.

I sat with Tom and a couple of other players for a while, shootin' the breeze and talking about different things that went on back in St. Louis. The Cardinals pitching coach was my high school soccer coach, and so we were talking about that. Time started to get away from us, and after having a few drinks, we headed home.

The next day at the ballpark, Tom was giving me some trouble, saying that I was a real sloppy drunk and making a scene late last night. This was very untrue, but he was just trying to scare me a bit.

When we got back to Arkansas after the series was over, Tom was two days away from going home. The first day we were back, we were hitting batting practice when two cops showed up and sat in the grandstand watching us. To put a little fear in me, one of the players made a comment that the two cops were there for me for acting silly at the bar in Louisiana. I told him that I didn't do anything and that I was fine that night.

The next night, which was the night Tom was leaving, he bought everyone dinner after the game. I sat in the stands to do the radar gun. I was in jeans and a T-shirt and just went up to the clubhouse after the game. I knocked on the door, put the radar gun down, and grabbed a steak and salad. I sat in front of my locker and started to eat when two guys started beating down the clubhouse door like they were going to kick it in. Two cops walked in and went straight back to the manager's office. At this time, Pagnozzi was nowhere to be found. He was hiding in the training room.

The two cops came out with the manager, who pointed right at me and said, "That's the guy right there." The two cops walked over. By now, I am just trying to eat my steak. I was scared and shaking. The cops asked me, "Is your name Cliff Politte?" and I said "Yes sir." They then said, "Will you please put your food down? You're under arrest." I asked them for what, and they said, "For acting disorderly at a bar and for disturbing the peace."

We had a soda machine in the clubhouse, and I was face-first against it. They were frisking my body and found my car keys in my pocket. One cop asked if the keys were a pocketknife, and I told him that they were just my keys.

In Little Rock, there were two sets of doors between the clubhouse exit and the exit outside where fans wait for you. The cops now had me between these swinging doors. There was a payphone there, and I asked if I could make a phone call. I was pale white. Everyone in the clubhouse was serious because everyone was in on the joke.

The cops said that I couldn't use the payphone and that I could make a call from downtown. I started thinking that my dad was going to kill me and the Cardinals were going to release me. Just before we got outside, one of the cops looked at me and said, "I just want to let you know that we are just messing around and that someone has pulled a joke on you."

I almost started bawling. I was so scared, sweaty, and nervous. The cop un-handcuffed me and let me go back to my locker. Pagnozzi came out of the back with a big smile on his face and said, "I got you!"

That was probably the funniest thing that has ever happened to me. My teammates were rolling. They were all in on it since the time that we left Shreveport. It ended up making the *Post Dispatch* newspaper in St. Louis, with a story about how the local kid got pranked by a big leaguer. It was really great.

Marcus Thames

Major League Clubs/
Minor League Organizations:
NEW YORK YANKEES, TEXAS RANGERS,
DETROIT TIGERS

Position: OUTFIELDER

Team: NORWICH, CT

League: EASTERN

Year: 1999

MARCUS THAMES blasted himself into the record books when he became the nineteenth player in Major League baseball to hit a home run on his first big league pitch on June 10, 2002. More impressively, Thames's homer came off of future Hall of Famer Randy Johnson in a rematch of the 2001 World Series in front of a capacity crowd at Yankee Stadium.

Thames played parts of eight seasons in the Minor Leagues from 1997 to 2004. His memorable Minor League experience occurred while playing Class AA ball in the New York Yankees organization.

I will never forget Mother's Day in 1999. I talked to my Mom that morning, and she told me to hit a home run for her that day. I told her that I would try.

In my second at-bat, I hit a grand slam, the first grand slam of my career, against Bowie in Norwich. After I hit it and was rounding the bases, I realized that I actually did it.

I called her after the game and first asked her how she was doing. Then, I said, "Guess what? I hit a grand slam, not just a home run. I hit a grand slam just for you."

She was very excited about it. It was one of the most meaningful home runs for me.

Toby Hall

Major League Clubs/Minor League Organizations:
TAMPA BAY DEVIL RAYS

Position: CATCHER

Team: ORLANDO, FL

League: SOUTHERN

Year: 1999

TOBY HALL reached the Major Leagues in 2000 and became Tampa Bay's everyday catcher by the end of the following year. In five Major League seasons, he has become recognized as one of the best defensive catchers in the game by throwing out a combined 40 percent would-be base stealers.

Hall played parts of six seasons in the Minor Leagues from 1997 to 2002. His memorable Minor League experience occurred while playing Class AA ball in the Tampa Bay Devil Rays organization.

It was game 4 of the best-of-five Southern League Championship Series, and we were leading two games to one against the West Tenn Diamond Jaxx.

I was already having a great series, hitting a two-out, bases-clearing double in the first inning of game 3 in a 4–3 win in Jackson, Tennessee.

Down 3–1 in the fourth inning, I was at the plate when we were starting to rally. With a 2–2 pitch on the way, I swung and sharply fouled the ball off of my left leg. Immediately, I fell to the dirt in agonizing pain.

My manager Bill Russell and the trainer quickly came out of the dugout to look at me. I thought that I would have to come out of the game and be replaced by a pinch hitter. For ten minutes, the game was delayed as I sat in the right-hand batter's box having my leg examined.

The crowd was really quiet. The umpiring crew waited for a decision from Russell about me. Finally, I got up on my feet and convinced Russell to let me stay in the game. As I stepped back into the box, the crowd started to applaud and cheer.

With another 2–2 pitch on the way, I swung and lined a base hit to center field. West Tenn's center fielder scooped up the ball and saw that I was struggling to get to first base. I was running as best as I could, favoring my right leg to offset my injured left shin.

Then, about five feet away from first base, I fell hard to the ground. The center fielder fired the ball to first to try to get me and hold the Diamond Jaxx lead.

On my hands and knees, I crawled to first base and slapped my hand on the bag just before the ball got there. I was safe, and the rally continued!

I was replaced by pinch runner Paul Hoover, and we went on to score five runs in the inning on our way to a 10–3 win and the Southern League Championship. The game was the last ever played in the seventy-seven-year history of Tinker Field.

As we celebrated the title on the field, I was announced as the Most Valuable Player of the series. On crutches, I came out of the dugout to an ovation from our fans to accept the award and share the championship with my teammates.

I was later taken to an Orlando area hospital and found out that my left shin was broken.

Mike Lieberthal

Major League Clubs/Minor League Organizations:
PHILADELPHIA PHILLIES
Position: CATCHER
Team: SPARTANBURG/MARTINSVILLE
League: SOUTH ATLANTIC/APPALACHIAN
Year: 1991/1990

MIKE LIEBERTHAL has established himself as one of the premier catchers in the Major Leagues and Philadelphia Phillies history. In 1999, the two-time All-Star had a career year by hitting .300 with 31 home runs and 96 RBI. In addition, he earned his first Gold Glove Award that season. During his Phillies career, which started in the big leagues at twenty-two years old, he has hit .300 twice, belted 130 home runs, and collected over 500 RBI.

Lieberthal played parts of six seasons in the Minor Leagues from 1990 to 1995. His memorable Minor League experience occurred while playing Class A ball in the Philadelphia Phillies organization.

During my second year, I was kissed by Morganna [the Kissing Bandit] in Spartanburg while I was in the South Atlantic League.

She was big-time back then, doing the Major League scene and showing up at Minor League ballparks here and there.

I don't know where she ran out from, either the dugout or stands or something, while I was hitting. She just came up and gave me a kiss. It was pretty funny and the crowd liked it.

I knew she was at the game, everybody did. Every player knew it would be somebody but no one knew who. It was great but a little embarrassing. It was exciting.

But the hardest year in the minors was probably my first year, which was in Martinsville. I struggled there and started thinking about how I could have gone to school and stuff like that.

But, my option was pretty easy, because I was drafted third overall in the first round and got a lot of money. I knew that if I was drafted in the first two rounds that I would sign.

In Martinsville, I lived with a family and two other guys. We stayed upstairs in a little room. It was a great family that I lived with. I would talk to them a lot about things that year. They were great people and took in players every year.

I actually still see them because they come to Philadelphia games once in a while.

Johnny Pesky

Major League Clubs/Minor League Organizations:
BOSTON RED SOX, DETROIT TIGERS,
WASHINGTON SENATORS
Position: SHORTSTOP/MANAGER
Team: ROCKY MOUNT, NC
League: CAROLINA
Year: 1940

JOHNNY PESKY has been associated with the Boston Red Sox for more than sixty years. The All-Star shortstop batted .320 for Boston and finished his ten-year career with a .307 average. Pesky is one of three players in Major League baseball history to collect 200 hits in his first three seasons, accomplishing the feat in 1942 and 1946–1947. He spent 1943–1945 serving his country during World War II in the United States Armed Forces. One of the most admired Sox players ever, the right field foul pole at Fenway Park is nicknamed "Pesky's Pole."

Pesky played two seasons in the Minor Leagues from 1940 to 1941. His memorable Minor League experience occurred while playing Class A, B and AAA ball in the Boston Red Sox organization.

My first year was in 1940, but I signed in 1939 and didn't start playing right away.

I was eighteen years old when I signed and the next year at nineteen, they sent me to Rocky Mount, North Carolina. I got $500 when I signed in 1939. We were still in the depression and that was a lot of money then. In those years, there was no baseball draft and you could sign with anybody. The scouts would come and watch us play in high school and then in tournaments.

I had two or three clubs that talked to me to sign. My mother liked the guy from Boston. I got an offer from another organization for $1,500, but my mother said that she didn't care about the money because she knew Mr. Johnson would take care of me. I didn't really care because I just wanted to play. So, I signed with them and I'm glad that I did. I have so much respect for the Red Sox and will always have special feelings for the Red Sox.

My first manager was Heinie Manush in Class B ball and I had a good year. I led the league in hits and later that year, Heinie wanted me to go to Boston. I told him that I was getting homesick but he wanted me to go up so that they could get a look at me. I never dreamed that I would even go to the American Association. I went to the Louisville team the next year and had another good year. I was in the All-Star Game and was the Most Valuable Player in the league. I led the league in hits again and then I went to Boston.

We used to get great crowds and drew very well in Louisville. The players were very good, too. In fact, in the American Association in 1941, all eight shortstops went to the big leagues.

In that kind of a league, there were a lot of veteran players. In those years, you just didn't move that much. We had Class D clubs, C clubs, B clubs, A, A-1, AA, and AAA. We had something like sixteen clubs with a team in Little Rock, Virginia, Carolina, and more.

But when you go through all of that and see all of that, what you learned to do was to play ball.

Pete Walker

Major League Clubs/Minor League
Organizations: NEW YORK METS,
SAN DIEGO PADRES, BOSTON RED SOX,
COLORADO ROCKIES, TORONTO
BLUE JAYS

Position: PITCHER

Team: COLORADO SPRINGS, CO

League: PACIFIC COAST

Year: 1999

PETE WALKER earned his spot in the Major Leagues after years of hard work and determination. After reaching the big leagues in 1995 with the New York Mets and pitching in 13 games that year, Walker appeared in only four more Major League games over the next six seasons. A candidate for Comeback Player of the Year in 2002 with the Toronto Blue Jays, Pete went 10–5 with a solid 4.33 ERA in 20 starts and 37 games in his most productive professional season.

Walker spent parts of fourteen seasons in the Minor Leagues from 1990 to 2003. His memorable Minor League experience occurred while playing Class AAA ball in the Colorado Rockies organization.

My most distinctive memories of the Minor Leagues were the many hellos and goodbyes to family and friends over the years.

One that topped the list was in June of 1999 in Colorado Springs. I was playing Triple-A ball for the Sky Sox of the Colorado Rockies organization. After breaking into the Major League with the New York Mets in 1995, my career had taken a major nosedive. A shoulder surgery in 1996 and knee surgery in 1998 all but put me out of the game.

The Rockies gave me an opportunity in 1999 to get back on track, but I was still going nowhere fast. I was away from wife, Kari, who supported me in my endeavor to get back to the big leagues, and was away from my three-year-old daughter Kazi. We have since added two girls to the pack, Marissa and Milena.

I had been away from Kari and Kazi for almost two months. Obviously, it was long enough to contemplate retirement on an hourly basis. It was very difficult being away and not being able to be with them every day. Playing in the Minor Leagues with a family was no easy task.

I remember when they finally arrived from Connecticut. It was during a game and I was in the bullpen. I saw them both at the top of the entranceway to the stadium. But that wasn't going to do. Kazi squirmed out of my wife's arms and charged down the grassy hill toward the bullpen.

With a capacity crowd, you can imagine that there were definitely some people watching her run down the hill. I had to meet her halfway up the hill, in full uniform, to keep her from taking a nasty spill. She squeezed me with all of her might, and I did all that I could do to keep from tearing up.

Little does she know, that moment resurrected my career and gave me the strength to keep battling. I will never forget her sprinting down the hill.

With every hello, there was a goodbye. Two weeks later, it was time for my girls to go back home. The airport scene was not a good one. Although I did everything that I could do to keep Kazi excited about her airplane trip, she was convinced that I was going, too.

When she realized that I wasn't, she chased after me, threw herself to the airport carpet and screamed, "Daddy, Daddy." Again, I contemplated retirement for the umpteenth time. However, I was able to persevere through the rest of that season and played very well in the second half of the season.

I got back to the big leagues the following season with the Rockies, and then went on to the Mets in 2001 and the Blue Jays in 2002 and 2003.

Alex Rodriguez

Major League Clubs/Minor League
Organizations: SEATTLE MARINERS,
 TEXAS RANGERS, NEW YORK YANKEES

Position: SHORTSTOP, THIRD BASE

Team: APPLETON, WI

League: MIDWEST

Year: 1994

ALEX RODRIGUEZ is one of the most productive players ever in Major League baseball. The eight-time All-Star reached the big leagues at nineteen years old and has a career batting average of .305 with 381 home runs and 1,109 RBI in his first eleven seasons. The 2003 American League MVP is one of only three players in Major League history to hit at least 40 home runs and steal 40 bases in the same season. Rodriguez posted back-to-back 50-plus home run and 135-plus RBI seasons in 2001 and 2002 with Texas, while becoming the youngest player in baseball to hit 300 home runs.

Rodriguez played parts of three seasons in the Minor Leagues from 1994 to 1996. His memorable Minor League experience occurred while playing Class A ball in the Seattle Mariners organization.

I remember the Minor Leagues as being a culture shock. All of my peers were going to college and I was going to the Minor Leagues.

My whole life, I always planned on going to college. I looked at going into the Minor Leagues like me going away to college. That was my way of staying motivated and not really getting homesick. Either I go to the Minor Leagues, or I go to "Wisconsin University." I was still going to be away from home.

The culture shock for me was being in Appleton, Wisconsin, and being away from home. Having my own apartment with a roommate and having to pay rent. Playing in the middle of snow in April and saying, "Holy crap! What did I sign up for?"

I had a brand new Cherokee that I bought with my signing bonus. I thought that was like a Bentley and was the greatest thing in the world.

I remember hanging out with the boys, buying pizzas, going to the malls, and on every Friday night, all of the boys getting together to have a few drinks at a bar.

Well, I almost got arrested because I tried to sneak in a couple times and was only eighteen.

They wouldn't let me in. So, I got a fake ID and got in on a couple of Fridays. Finally, on the third Friday, the cops got me outside and almost arrested me. They realized I was Alex, and Appleton was a small town.

That was funny, I almost got arrested.

Steve Trachsel

Major League Clubs/Minor League Organizations: CHICAGO CUBS, TAMPA BAY DEVIL RAYS, NEW YORK METS

Position: PITCHER

Team: IOWA

League: AMERICAN ASSOCIATION

Year: 1993

STEVE TRACHSEL is one of the most durable starting pitchers in the big leagues over the past ten years. Since 1994, he has started at least 22 games every season and at least 30 games six times over that span. An All-Star in 1996 with Chicago, he helped guide the Cubs into the playoffs in 1998 by winning 15 games. In 2003, he posted his best season by going 16–10 with a 3.78 ERA with the New York Mets.

Trachsel played parts of four seasons in the Minor Leagues from 1991 to 1994. His memorable Minor League experience occurred while playing Class AAA ball in the Chicago Cubs organization.

It was 1993 and I was in Triple-A with the Iowa Cubs.

We were in the playoffs and I think that I pitched in Game 6. We went to Game 7, and it was just like everyone writes it. I got there early to pack up my stuff because I knew that I was going home either way.

The manager, Marv Foley, called me in to his office and told me that after the game I was going up to Chicago. I was thinking, "Awesome." I had never been to the big leagues before, not even for big league spring training or anything. I said, "This is great."

But, he then told me that there was a problem. He said that I couldn't tell anybody until after the game.

So, I've got Game 7 of the championship, I'm going to the big leagues, and couldn't tell anybody. He said that there were eight other guys going with me, and he hasn't told any of them yet.

By now, I was thinking that he probably should have waited until after the game to tell me. Some of the guys that went up with me were Eddie Zambrano, Turk Wendell, Blaise Ilsley, Kevin Roberson, and a couple others.

We ended up winning the game, partied until 4 A.M., packed up the truck at 8 A.M., closed out the lease on the apartment, and drove to Chicago.

Ellis Burks

Major League Clubs/Minor League Organizations:
BOSTON RED SOX, CHICAGO WHITE SOX, COLORADO ROCKIES,
SAN FRANCISCO GIANTS, CLEVELAND INDIANS

Position: CENTER FIELD

Team: WINTER HAVEN, FL

League: SPRING TRAINING

Year: 1984

ELLIS BURKS was one of the most productive, consistent, and professional players in baseball during his career. In eighteen big league seasons, he batted .291 with 352 home runs, 1,206 RBI, and hit 20 or more home runs eight times. The two-time All-Star and Gold Glove winner had his best season in 1996 with Colorado, batting .344 with 40 home runs and 128 RBI.

Burks played parts of five seasons in the Minor Leagues from 1983 to 1987. His memorable Minor League experience occurred while playing Class A ball in the Boston Red Sox organization.

I was in A ball in my second Minor League spring training with the Red Sox when I had the honor of meeting Ted Williams.

He came up to me and said, "Son, what's your name?" I said, "My name is Ellis Burks, sir. It's nice to meet you."

He introduced himself and told me that I had a hell of a bat and that the ball jumped off my bat. He said that he liked the way the ball carried off of my bat.

He then asked me, "Do you have an agent?" I said, "No, sir." He said, "Well, I want to be your agent!"

He said it jokingly, but I thought he was serious. He had a serious look on his face. I called my Mom and Dad that night and told them that Ted Williams said he wanted to be my agent.

Well, I heard him say that to someone else two days later. I put it together and figured out that was what he said to a guy that he enjoyed watching or thought had the chance to play at the big league level.

It was what he told most of the prospects that he liked at that time to motivate and encourage them. It really encouraged me because to hear that from him was wonderful.

Jeff Clark

Major League Clubs/Minor League Organizations:
SAN FRANCISCO GIANTS

Position: PITCHER

Team: NORWICH, CT

League: EASTERN

Year: 2003

JEFF CLARK was selected in the twentieth round of the 2000 June draft by the San Francisco Giants. Still striving to reach the Major Leagues, he has won 36 games in five Minor League seasons and has recorded 415 strike-outs in 491 innings pitched. A native of eastern Connecticut, he grew up watching the local Minor League baseball team in Norwich, Connecticut.

Clark has played five seasons in the Minor Leagues from 2000 to 2004. His memorable Minor League experience occurred while playing Class AA ball in the San Francisco Giants organization.

In 2002, I was the California League Pitcher of the Year with high hopes in my career of moving up the chain in the Giants organization. Near the end of 2002, I was promoted to Double-A in Shreveport, Louisiana.

At the end of that year, Shreveport's contract with the Giants had terminated, and San Francisco signed with Norwich, Connecticut. Being from nearby Ledyard, Connecticut, I knew that I would be one of the first players from the area to have the rare chance to play for Norwich.

Everything was going well, and I was excited to begin the season so close to home after I made the Double-A team to start 2003. But I struggled the first month and ended up getting hurt, breaking my foot while doing some conditioning. I was out for nine weeks, the longest nine weeks of my life, and was sent to Single-A when I came back. I still struggled there and started to think that my career could be over just as quickly as it started.

I was lucky enough that the Giants called me back up to Double-A, and I got to pitch in three more games there. My first game I did well, but it was my second start that was the most memorable one. It was my first home game since I got hurt, and threw 7.2 innings of two-hit, shutout ball. I ended up getting the win.

As I left the field, I got a standing ovation. It was pretty memorable because it was the home crowd, and the feeling that was going through my body was indescribable.

I just felt bad because I didn't acknowledge the crowd from being too nervous of what my teammates would say about me for being the hometown kid.

Rocco Baldelli

Major League Clubs/Minor League Organizations: TAMPA BAY DEVIL RAYS
Position: CENTER FIELD
Team: PRINCETON, WV
League: APPALACHIAN
Year: 2000

ROCCO BALDELLI is well on his way to being the next superstar center fielder in Major League baseball. In his first two seasons with the Tampa Bay Devil Rays, he batted .285 with 27 home runs, 152 RBI, and 44 stolen bases. In 2003, Baldelli made his big league debut at just twenty-two years old and finished third in the voting for the American League Rookie of the Year award.

Baldelli played three seasons in the Minor Leagues from 2000 to 2002. His memorable Minor League experience occurred while playing Class A ball in the Tampa Bay Devil Rays organization.

I flew out to Princeton, West Virginia, with one other guy on this little fifteen-passenger plane. There wasn't really much to the town. It was a kind of small town in West Virginia.

I showed up to the field, walked into the clubhouse and saw two of my teammates fighting. They were going at it, not punching each other, but were in each others faces about something.

I hadn't seen a fight in a long time. It was pretty weird to walk in and have the first thing you see be two guys going at it. I didn't say anything and just walked over to meet the manager.

I didn't have too many big moments my first year. I remember basically every hit that I had the entire season. I have it stored in memory. I hit about .215 that year with three home runs. I was pretty miserable and wasn't too happy about playing. I pretty much wanted to go home.

Being away from home was a big adjustment. I grew up in Rhode Island and have always been kind of a homebody. I was always with my family, and everything that I did was with my family, so going away and being away from them for six or eight months at a time was probably one of the toughest transitions for me.

My first year was pretty bad overall. Everything about it was just horrible. I couldn't think of one good thing about my season. I think that the off-season was huge. Whenever you had four months off to just relax and not have to think about baseball, it recharged you for the next year.

My third year, I started out in Bakersfield, California, and went to Double-A and then Triple-A in one year. That was when I started to believe in myself that I could get it done. There were so many coaches that helped me along the way.

A lot of those guys in the Minor Leagues, whether they are instructors, coaches, or managers, give their lives and do not get the recognition that they deserve. Those were the guys that I spent hundreds of hours on the field getting better with.

Fred Lynn

Major League Clubs/Minor League
Organizations: BOSTON RED SOX,
CALIFORNIA ANGELS, BALTIMORE
ORIOLES, DETROIT TIGERS,
SAN DIEGO PADRES

Position: OUTFIELDER

Team: PAWTUCKET, RI

League: INTERNATIONAL

Year: 1974

FRED LYNN played seventeen seasons in the Major Leagues with five teams and was a nine-time All-Star. He won the Most Valuable Player award in 1975 as well as the 1975 Rookie of the Year. In his career, he hit 306 home runs, collected 1,111 RBI, and had a lifetime batting average of .283. Defensively, Lynn won five Gold Glove Awards.

Lynn played parts of five seasons in the Minor Leagues from 1970 to 1975. His memorable Minor League experience occurred while playing Class AAA ball in the Boston Red Sox organization.

The one thing about Minor League baseball that I can recall was how much I disliked it.

I came from the University of Southern California, where we flew just about everywhere that we went and stayed in the best hotels. We won three national championships when I was there, so I was used to winning, good travel conditions, good playing conditions, towels, soap, and those kinds of things.

When I got to the Minor Leagues, those things weren't there. Especially in Triple-A, where I thought it was a league that we were supposed to fly everywhere. We went on a road trip that was written up in *The Sporting News* as the road trip from hell.

We went from Pawtucket to Toledo, which was fifteen or sixteen hours, got off the bus, and took infield about ten minutes later. I remember that I pulled a hamstring muscle during that time and played only one game on the trip.

I am not quite sure of the sequence of the trip, but we went from something like Toledo to Memphis, Memphis to Richmond, Richmond to somewhere else, and then back to Pawtucket. The road trip was about fifteen days in four cities, and each leg of the trip was fifteen or sixteen hours.

I know that we won only one game on the whole trip, and I don't think our owners cared very much about it either because we were 30 games out and 30 games under .500. I remember guys trying to sleep in the baggage compartments of the bus. These were not big, fancy buses or anything. They were just regular buses. Guys 6'5", 240 pounds were squeezing into these little luggage racks where you would put your Walkman for a sixteen-hour bus ride.

I wanted to get out of the Minor Leagues really badly. In fact, when we were out in Toledo, I was talking to one of the umpires about that. It was Ken Kaiser, who went up to the big leagues, too. I told him, "Kenny, I have had enough of this and going to quit. I am going to go back, finish out my education, and go into teaching like I wanted to do in the first place."

Ken went up to the big leagues the same year that I did in 1975. I came up to the plate in a game that he was umpiring when he said, "Hey kid, do you still want to go back to do a little of that teaching now?" I was hitting about .340 at the time and just turned and gave him a smile.

I was in a real big hurry to get out of the Minor Leagues because I didn't like any of it.

Larry Andersen

Major League Clubs/Minor League Organizations:
CLEVELAND INDIANS, SEATTLE MARINERS,
PHILADELPHIA PHILLIES, HOUSTON ASTROS,
BOSTON RED SOX, SAN DIEGO PADRES

Position: PITCHER

Team: SARASOTA, FL

League: FLORIDA STATE

Year: 1971

LARRY ANDERSEN was a solid big league middle reliever and closer during his seventeen-year career, compiling a 40–39 record with a 3.15 ERA in 699 games. He pitched in two World Series with the Philadelphia Phillies and three Championship Series with Philadelphia, Boston, and Houston. In 1986 with the Astros in the NLCS, he fired five scoreless innings of one-hit ball in two appearances against the New York Mets.

Anderson played parts of ten seasons in the Minor Leagues from 1971 to 1981. His memorable Minor League experience occurred while playing Class A ball in the Cleveland Indians organization.

It was my first year in rookie ball in Sarasota, Florida.

I was living with four other guys, and we bought a 1962 Ford Falcon. That was our transportation to the ballpark. We lived on Tamiami Trail on Siesta Key.

One day, it was pouring out so bad that the streets were flooded. We got in our Falcon and the water was so high, it killed our engine. We were all sitting there talking and decided that there was no way that we were playing.

So, we left the car, went back to our apartment and kicked back. Come to find out, it stopped raining at the ballpark, dried up, and they played the game. There were five no-shows.

It's one of those things that you don't not show up for a game. We did not show up for the game.

That was a big lesson for me right from the get-go. We got a stern lecture from Lenny Johnston, who was our manager, as well as a $40 fine for each of us. We were making all of $500 per month and after taxes were clearing about $200 of that every two weeks. So, $40 was about 20 percent of your salary. Since then, I didn't care what the situation was, I would be at the ballpark for a game.

In rookie ball, Lenny also said something which had a lasting effect on me. He said, "I don't know which of you guys are going to make it to the big leagues and which of you aren't. But, for those of you that make it, if you don't remember anything else, remember this . . . You are going to meet the same people on your way down that you meet on the way up. And depending upon how you treat those people on your way up is going to determine how they will treat you on your way down."

I have never forgotten that.

Mark Prior

Major League Clubs/Minor League
Organizations: CHICAGO CUBS

Position: PITCHER

Team: JACKSON, TN

League: SOUTHERN

Year: 2002

MARK PRIOR broke into the Major Leagues with the Chicago Cubs at just twenty-two years old after only nine starts in the Minor Leagues. In his first full season in 2003, he earned a spot on the All-Star team by going 18–6 with a 2.43 ERA and 245 strikeouts over 211.1 innings pitched. The second overall pick in the 2001 June draft, Prior led the Cubs to the postseason in '03 and was 2–1 with a 2.35 ERA in three starts against the Atlanta Braves and Florida Marlins.

Prior played less than one season in the Minor Leagues in 2002. His memorable Minor League experience occurred while playing Class AA ball in the Chicago Cubs organization.

I was in Double-A in Jackson, Tennessee, and it was the fourth or fifth inning.

They had a petting zoo out in right field, and would let donkeys on the warning track during the game in between innings. Unfortunately, it took the donkey more than the ninety seconds it was allowed to get off the field.

So, we all had to sit and wait another two or three minutes for this donkey to make it to the other side of the fence.

It was pretty funny, these donkeys walking out on the warning track giving rides to kids. But, that's all I really remember.

Brook Fordyce

Major League Clubs/Minor League Organizations:
NEW YORK METS, BALTIMORE ORIOLES,
TAMPA BAY DEVIL RAYS, CHICAGO WHITE SOX,
CINCINNATI REDS

Position: CATCHER

Team: BINGHAMTON, NY

League: EASTERN

Year: 1992

BROOK FORDYCE has put together a very solid career as a Major League catcher. Although he has spent most of his time as a reserve, Fordyce flourished in his role as a starter with the Chicago White Sox in 1999 by batting .297 with nine home runs and 49 RBI. Over the past ten seasons, he has played in 623 games, collecting 41 home runs and 188 RBI.

Fordyce played parts of eleven seasons in the Minor Leagues from 1989 to 2000. His memorable Minor League experience occurred while playing Class AA ball in the New York Mets organization.

I played on a championship team in 1992 with the Binghamton Mets.

I almost forgot about that because I am so far from it now. That may have been the greatest season ever, because we just kept winning and winning and it came down to one game. After 142 games, we played one game to win it. Even though it was just a Minor League championship, it was pretty special.

The Minor Leagues were great for me because it formed my character and mental toughness. I put six years in, and it was peaks and valleys. But the peaks and valleys were a lot more extreme down there. Everything seemed like sudden death. The overall Minor League experience made me a better player up here.

The grind of playing 142 games, going to the instructional league, and then playing winter ball was the toughest part of the

Minor Leagues. I was playing baseball all year-round, and I did that for almost six straight years. There was no rest, and I wondered how my body took that. I gave everything I had just to get that chance of chasing the dream to play in the big leagues.

I always thought that I would make it. My determination and drive was unbelievable to get there. I didn't know when I was going to get there, but that I would get there.

But the best part of the Minor Leagues were the friendships formed because everybody was in it to get to one place, which was the big leagues.

We would pull pranks on one other. A friend of mine from Connecticut, Hal Winslow, once called my teammate Pete Walker and paid him to take my clothes and my paycheck and hide them from me.

After the game, I came in and everyone had showered and left. I was still looking for my clothes. I looked up at my name and it said, "Hal Winslow strikes again!" I found out that it was Pete who hid my clothes. He hid them in the freezer or something.

I wasn't worried about my clothes as much as my paycheck in them.

Jim Thome

Major League Clubs/Minor League
Organizations: PHILADELPHIA PHILLIES,
CLEVELAND INDIANS

Position: FIRST BASE

Team: BURLINGTON, NC

League: CAROLINA

Year: 1990

JIM THOME is one of the best power-hitting first basemen in the history of baseball. In fourteen seasons, he has blasted 423 home runs, accumulated more than 1,163 RBI, and has a lifetime batting average of .285. His best overall season was in 2002 with the Indians, when he launched 52 homers, collected 118 RBI, and batted .304. The four-time All-Star has hit 40 or more home runs five times and has driven in 100-plus runs eight times in his career.

Thome played parts of five seasons in the Minor Leagues from 1989 to 1993. His memorable Minor League experience occurred while playing Class A, AA, and AAA ball in the Cleveland Indians organization.

For me, all of the bus trips were always memorable at each level. You really got close to your teammates that way. I always remember that camaraderie built with your teammates on those twelve- or fifteen-hour trips. Guys would play cards to pass the time. They were cooped up in a bus going on a long trip. On top of that, when you got into the cities, you always had roommates in the Minor Leagues.

You spent a lot of time with your teammates, even when stopping late at night at Wendy's or McDonald's. Meal money was not much then, $8 or $9, if that. But, you were all working hard to get to where we are now.

Charlie Manuel really helped me get to the big leagues. He was our roving hitting instructor until I got to Triple-A. When I got to Triple-A, he was my manager. I always spent time with him each year. I had a week in Burlington, North Carolina, in Short-A ball where I had a really good week. I hit five, six, or seven home runs that week. Back then, I didn't hit a lot of home runs. I always remember that week maybe being my jump start. I didn't become a home run hitter until I got to the big leagues. He was the one guy, as I look back, that I would say had the most effect on my career.

But what stood out to me in the minors were the leagues. I remember in Bristol, Tennessee, they had a hillside in right field that made it look like you were playing in the woods.

I also remember in Double-A, Canton-Akron was our home field and it was run in a big-league style. They took a lot of pride in that because it was an hour from Cleveland and a lot of the brass would come down. We had players there like Brian Giles and Arthur Rhodes.

Then, in Triple-A, the Braves had Chipper Jones, Javy Lopez, Mark Wohlers, and Ryan Klesko. I remember Charlotte being a great place to play. I always loved Charlotte. The people were friendly and the ballpark was great to hit in.

Really, all of Minor League experiences were great. They really were.

John Franco

Major League Clubs/Minor League Organizations:
LOS ANGELES DODGERS, CINCINNATI REDS,
NEW YORK METS
Position: PITCHER
Team: SAN ANTONIO, TX
League: TEXAS
Year: 1982

JOHN FRANCO is one of the best relief pitchers ever and is the National League all-time leader in saves with 424. The five-time All-Star, who has fired 1,230 innings in 1,088 games over twenty Major League seasons, has posted at least 25 saves in eleven of those years. In five post-season series with the New York Mets, Franco was 2–0 in 15 games with a 1.88 ERA.

Franco played parts of four seasons in the Minor Leagues from 1981 to 1984. His memorable Minor League experience occurred while playing Class AA ball in the Los Angeles organization.

I think the best time in my life in the Minor Leagues was in Double-A in San Antonio, Texas.

I had two roommates, one named Paul Voigt and another named Scotty Madison. The three of us had fun on the field and off the field. With the Dodgers in San Antonio, they bought a brand new, $750,000 customized bus that we traveled in the Texas League with. No matter how much the bus cost, it was still a bus ride of seventeen or eighteen hours.

With Paul and Scotty, they were just total opposites. Scotty was like Felix Unger, always keeping our place clean, while Paul and I were total slobs.

I remember we had a party at our house and the next day, Scotty went to the supermarket, met some older woman, and talked her into coming back to the apartment to clean up. He did this every time that we had a party at the house. We couldn't believe it.

We would have a keg party and Scotty would go around picking up the ashtrays, empty bottles, and sodas. We even had boxing matches in the house. We would go out every night and Paul would hand out San Antonio Dodgers schedules, telling people to come see us. There was always a party at our house but nobody would ever show up.

That was the closest-knit team that I could remember because our locker room was about the size of a shower stall. We had to get dressed in shifts there.

Richie Sexson

Major League Clubs/Minor League Organizations:
CLEVELAND INDIANS, MILWAUKEE BREWERS,
ARIZONA DIAMONDBACKS
Position: FIRST BASE
Team: COLUMBUS, GA
League: SOUTH ATLANTIC
Year: 1994

RICHIE SEXSON became one of the most dangerous power hitters in baseball after posting five straight 25-plus homer and 90-plus RBI seasons with Cleveland and Milwaukee from 1999 to 2003. In his last three seasons with the Brewers, he combined to hit 119 home runs and collect 351 RBI. The two-time All-Star twice tied the Brewers single-season home run record with 45 in 2001 and 2003.

Sexson played parts of six seasons in the Minor Leagues from 1993 to 1998. His memorable Minor League experience occurred while playing Class A ball in the Cleveland Indians organization.

It was in 1994 in Columbus, Georgia, in Low-A ball. Beautiful Low-A ball.

We were in the middle of a game, and I was hitting. Just as the pitcher was ready to throw the ball, a bolt of lightning came down and struck the light towers, shorting out all of the lights.

The pitch went by and the catcher, actually nobody, knew where it was. The pitch hit the backstop and the game was cancelled!

You don't know with lightning, if it's going to hit you or what. I will never forget that.

Ricky Bottalico

Major League Clubs/Minor League Organizations:
PHILADELPHIA PHILLIES, KANSAS CITY ROYALS,
ST. LOUIS CARDINALS, NEW YORK METS
Position: PITCHER
Team: SPARTANBURG, SC
League: SOUTH ATLANTIC
Year: 1992

RICKY BOTTALICO is a very dependable big league relief pitcher. During his eleven-year career, he has appeared in at least 60 games seven times and has averaged over 53 innings per season out of the bullpen. His best years were with the Philadelphia Phillies from 1996 to 1997, when he recorded back-to-back seasons of 34 saves.

Bottalico played parts of seven seasons in the Minor Leagues from 1991 to 2004. His memorable Minor League experience occurred while playing Class A ball in the Philadelphia Phillies organization.

One of the funniest things that I remember was when I was with Spartanburg in A ball. I was with the Phillies, and we would play in Charleston, South Carolina. Every time that we would go in there, they would have Hungry Thursdays or something. They would have quarter hot dogs. I will never forget this one day game, it was a Thursday, and we must have ordered about fifty hot dogs from the bullpen.

We just kept giving away baseballs to kids to go and get them for us. You think of it now, and you look at it and laugh, but back then it was like survival. We were hungry and wanted to eat. We were just crushing hot dogs during the game.

But the toughest part of it was getting drinks down there. We could have gotten some beer but I don't think that would have been the smartest thing in the world. There was a water cooler but you wanted a Coke!

We lost a lot of baseballs down there that day.

Then, also in Charlestown, West Virginia, I had never seen anybody make a sandwich so fast.

I don't know what the guy's name was, but we would always go to this Subway and this guy literally made a sandwich, cut the sandwich, and wrapped the sandwich in about twenty seconds every time.

It was the most unbelievable thing I had ever seen. He knocked out the entire team in five minutes. If you wanted a quick lunch, boom . . . Subway. He didn't go to the games or anything, we just knew him as "The Subway Guy." I'm not kidding, when I say that the whole team was in there, the whole team was in there.

It was funny things like that that made the Minor Leagues fun.

Eric Gagne

Major League Clubs/Minor League
Organizations: LOS ANGELES DODGERS

Position: PITCHER

Team: SAN ANTONIO, TX

League: TEXAS

Year: 1999

ERIC GAGNE has evolved into one of the greatest closers of all time. From 2002 to 2004, he set the record for most consecutive games saved with 84 and saved more than 50 games in each of those seasons. The three-time All-Star captured the 2003 National League Cy Young Award by converting 55 saves in 55 chances, while striking out 137 batters in 82.1 innings.

Gagne played parts of five seasons in the Minor Leagues from 1996 to 2001. His memorable Minor League experience occurred while playing Class AA ball in the Los Angeles Dodgers organization.

It was in 1999 and I was in Double-A.

I played the whole year there and I made the All-Star team. But, after that, I realized that I really couldn't see anything.

I couldn't see the signs at night, and I would cross up my catcher a lot. I would throw a fastball instead of a curveball and hit him right in the chest. I knew that there was something wrong with my eyes, so I went to get them checked out.

I found out that I had astigmatism and a few scars in my eyes. I got the scars from playing hockey. The doctor told me that I needed glasses because I couldn't see at night very well. With an astigmatism, everything that you look at is not really what you are seeing. It's like things are either far away or a little closer.

So, the first time that I wore my glasses, I wore them for a couple days before I had to start. When I finally did start, I did not throw one strike in three innings and they had to take me out. I couldn't find my release point and I was throwing everywhere.

It was pretty weird. For me, everything was different. I couldn't catch anything. I couldn't throw anything. I could barely walk!

For a couple of starts, I was really struggling. But after that, I was fine. It was the weirdest feeling I ever had in baseball.

Rick Wolff

Major League Clubs/Minor League Organizations:
DETROIT TIGERS, CHICAGO WHITE SOX

Position: SECOND BASE

Team: SOUTH BEND, IN

League: MIDWEST

Year: 1989

RICK WOLFF played two years in the Detroit Tigers Minor League system after being drafted out of Harvard. From 1990 to 1995, he worked as a roving coach for the Cleveland Indians, specializing in performance-enhancement skills and the mental approach to the game of baseball. Wolff was also the head baseball coach for eight years at Mercy College, a Division II program in New York, where several of his teams were nationally ranked. He is now a radio personality for WFAN 660 in New York.

Wolff played three seasons in the Minor Leagues from 1973 to 1974 and 1989. His memorable Minor League experience occurred while playing Class A ball in the Chicago White Sox organization.

It was 1989 and during a re-birth and re-interest in Minor League baseball.

The movie *Field of Dreams* was out and very popular. I was thirty-eight years old and had not played in the Minor Leagues since my mid-twenties. I hadn't even played any organized baseball for several years.

I was having a conversation one day with a friend at *Sports Illustrated*, who was an editor, and we were talking about the glamour of *Field of Dreams*. I was explaining to her that in the minors, the truth was that there are a lot of 0-for-4s, ten-hour bus rides, a lot of loneliness, and a lot of frustration that most fans are unaware of. It is a tough, tough existence.

So, she said to me, "Why don't you go back to the Midwest League, in Iowa and the cornfields, work out a deal to be a player, and write about how difficult and tough it is?"

I told her that I would be more than happy to do that, but it was hard enough getting signed when I was twenty-one. Getting a contract at age thirty-eight would be impossible. She told me that was the deal.

I made a bunch of phone calls and contacted an old buddy of mine named Al Goldis, who was the top scout of the Chicago White Sox. He once coached me when I played in the Atlantic Collegiate Baseball League.

He said to me that the South Bend White Sox of the Midwest League had clinched the first half of the season and had seven games in hand. If I wanted to get out there, and that I would sign an insurance waiver that I wouldn't sue them if I got hurt, they would get me signed.

I went back to my friend at *SI* and told her the deal. She told me to get out there, get in uniform, and get playing. She then reiterated to me that I had to play, not just be a first-base coach, and get into the games.

I went out and joined the South Bend team. I was there for three days and got into the game my first day that I was there. We were playing the Burlington, Iowa Braves, the Class A team of the Atlanta Braves. They had some kid throwing 90 miles per hour. I got a bat and was thinking that if I struck out, it was no big deal. However, I was thrilled and amazed because I grounded out to the shortstop. I was 0-for-1.

The next day, they actually started me. As my time there developed in the course of the next two days, with the pitchers from Burlington throwing anywhere from the low 90s to the mid-90s, I ended up going 4-for-7 with three RBI. In my last at-bat, I doubled off of the center field wall. For some reason, the ball was real easy to see. Perhaps it was because of the fear involved.

I will never forget playing second base next to a nineteen-year-old shortstop, and my glove was older than he was.

The manager was Rick Patterson, who was about thirty-four years old. He was four years younger than I was. At first, he was not happy about me being there because he was afraid that I would kill myself. But by the third day, he was my biggest fan and wondering how I was getting hits and doing so well.

It was a glorious situation. My family came out to South Bend with me. My wife, Trish, was right there in the front row and led the cheers with my children. My last day there, the mayor came out and gave me the keys to the city.

The South Bend White Sox ended up winning all three games and went on to win the season championship. At the end of the year, the team voted me a championship ring because I was their unofficial leading hitter for the season, batting .571.

The following year, the team had me go back out on Opening Day to receive my ring and throw out the first pitch of the season.

I wrote a long piece for *Sports Illustrated*, which ran that fall and got tremendous attention. The irony of writing the piece was that I was supposed to go there and write about how tough and frustrating it was in the minors.

I called the editor and told her that I had an unusual story to tell about my life in South Bend. The angle of the piece turned out to be about this dream, fantasy situation.

About four or five years later, I was forty-three years old and working for the Cleveland Indians as a roving sports psychology coach. One day, the Chicago White Sox were playing in Cleveland and taking batting practice. I was on the field and in uniform.

A left-handed pitcher named Scott Radinsky, who pitched for the White Sox and played for South Bend while I was there, saw me in an Indians uniform. He looked at me, came over and asked me if I was now playing for the Indians?

He really made my day.

Doug Glanville

Major League Clubs/Minor League Organizations:
PHILADELPHIA PHILLIES, CHICAGO CUBS, TEXAS RANGERS
Position: OUTFIELDER
Team: WINSTON-SALEM, NC
League: CAROLINA
Year: 1992

DOUG GLANVILLE has been the spark plug at the top of the line-up for every team he has played for. Over his nine-year career, he has been a solid overall producer with a .280 career batting average, 168 stolen bases, and 32 triples. His best season came in 1999 with the Phillies, when he hit .325 with 11 home runs, 73 RBI, and 34 stolen bases.

Glanville played six seasons in the Minor Leagues from 1991 to 1996. His memorable Minor League experience occurred while playing Class A ball in the Chicago Cubs organization.

There was this one character that I played with and his name was Ben Burlingame.

He was our comic relief in the Carolina League when we played for Winston-Salem, which was then named the Spirit and the Cubs affiliate in High-A ball. He was the clown of the team and always had something going on.

One story that stood out was on the road. There was a 10K run for some charity that was ending at home plate. The final few yards of the run went around the outfield warning track and ended at home plate.

Well, he heard about this run. So, he took his shirt off, wrote up a fake number and stuck it to his back. Just as the first five runners trying to win came around the corner, he jumped in the middle of race from the locker room.

He put on this show with his arms flailing and acting like he was going to pass out. He beat everybody, of course, because he only ran like one hundred yards. The guys were watching from the locker room and the field. We were cheering him on. The people in the race really had no idea who he was, and so they were trying to catch him but had nothing left. He just blew by them.

He collapsed at home plate, and we had to carry him off the field. The people at the finish line came running over with water. He was really playing it off. They didn't know who he was, either.

Finally, they figured out he was one of our players and that he wrote up a fake number, which was like 555. He kept everybody loose.

Ray Fagnant

Major League Clubs/Minor League Organizations:
PITTSBURGH PIRATES, BOSTON RED SOX

Position: CATCHER

Team: NEW BRITAIN, CT

League: EASTERN

Year: 1989

RAY FAGNANT has been a professional scout for the Boston Red Sox since 1993. Some of the players he signed include Marlins All-Star pitcher Carl Pavano, former Red Sox utility man Lou Merloni, and one-time Red Sox top pitching prospect Brian Rose. In 1999, he had a front-row seat at Fenway Park to slugger Mark McGwire's home run hitting display at the All-Star Game Home Run Derby. Fagnant was the catcher for the annual long ball contest.

Fagnant played six seasons in the Minor Leagues from 1987 to 1992. His memorable Minor League experience occurred while playing Class AA ball in the Boston Red Sox organization.

I signed with the Pittsburgh Pirates originally as a non-drafted free agent in 1987 out of Assumption College.

Then, halfway through the '88 season, I was one of the older guys doing okay but got released. The next spring, I called everybody because I still wanted to play. I had some good connections with the Red Sox because Bill Enos, their New England scout, saw me play so much during college.

Well, nothing worked out right away. So, that summer, I was working for Cigna in Hartford and played in a slow-pitch softball game on a Tuesday night. After the game, I said to my friend Jack, "Lets go see a New Britain Red Sox game tomorrow just for the heck of it."

The next day at work, I got a call from the Red Sox Minor League director saying that they needed a catcher and that I was the first guy that came to mind. Since it was June 21, 1989, I figured it would be in the Gulf Coast League or the New York-Penn League. I knew that they drafted Eric Wedge but had not signed him yet.

But he said, "We need you at New Britain tonight if you can make it."

He asked me about my job, because I had a full-time job as a consultant, and I said that I would do what I had to do and be there. I called my friend and told him that I would see him at the game tonight. I told him to meet me down by the bullpen before the game.

When I got to the field, I walked into the front office with a suit on and said, "I'm Ray. I'm the catcher." I then literally signed a contract on the desk of the general manager.

Butch Hobson was the manager, and he was one of my idols growing up. I had a picture taken with Butch at Fenway Park twelve or thirteen years earlier.

The team was going through a real bad slump. I got dressed and walked out to the dugout. Well, Butch took off his shirt and said, "I'm going out to the bullpen. If anyone wants to come out and fight me, let's go!" I was thinking, "Wow, this is a crazy team."

He then saw me and came over to introduce himself. He told me that they were going to get me in there that night.

My friend came down to the bullpen and couldn't believe it. He said, "I would like to say that stranger things have happened, but I really can't." The irony of the situation was that I had never been to a New Britain Red Sox game before.

I was the designated hitter that night and went 0-for-4. I put the ball in play three times.

The next day, I had to go back to work. When I walked in, I saw my boss right away. The first thing he said was, "What is zero divided by four?" He was breaking my chops for going 0-for-4.

That Friday night, thirty or forty people from Cigna, including many from the slow-pitch softball team, came to the game in New Britain. We played a doubleheader against the Harrisburg Senators, which was the Pirates affiliate then. It was pretty neat for me because I went to spring training the year before with many of the guys on that team.

Todd Pratt and I were the catchers. The Red Sox had a big catching prospect that had a sore arm, and so they put him on the disabled list. What was good was that they needed me because they played a lot of doubleheaders.

I was in New Britain for a couple of weeks, and when the prospect came off the DL, they sent me down to Florida. That was fine because I just wanted to stay in the organization.

Then, I played at three Minor League levels in a little more than twenty-four hours. I was in New Britain for an afternoon game, flew out to Florida early the next morning and played in a Gulf Coast League game that afternoon.

That was in Winter Haven, where the Gulf Coast League played at the Minor League complex and the Florida State League club played across the street at the big league spring training field.

After the game, I was in the clubhouse when Winter Haven manager Dave Holt came in to say that John Flaherty broke his hand the night before against Port Charlotte and that he needed a catcher. So, that night I made the trip to Lakeland to play against the Tigers in a doubleheader.

In the first game of the doubleheader, Paul Williams caught but I came in to catch the last couple of innings. Then, in the second game, Jack Morris was making a rehab start for Lakeland. He just had surgery and this was my debut for Winter Haven.

I was always more of a catch-and-throw guy. I probably led the league in batting practice home runs, but when the game started, I was a .180 hitter. I forgot that Morris was the winningest pitcher in baseball in the 1980s.

So, in my first at-bat, I got up, swung at the first pitch, and hit a double off the wall. In my second AB, I hit a home run. It was my only home run of the year.

In the seventh inning, which was the last inning of a doubleheader, they brought in a left-handed pitcher to face me. I was feeling good about myself because I had a home run and a double against Jack Morris. Well, I got jammed and hit a two-hopper to the shortstop to end the inning. I remember that we ended up losing the game.

The next day, I bought about twenty-five newspapers because I figured that years from now, I would have to prove my story.

In 2001, I was scouting in Ft. Pierce, Florida, watching a junior college game when I met up with Greg Morhardt, who is the New England scout for the New York Mets. Morhardt was a prolific hitter and a first-round draft pick out of the University of South Carolina.

While we were talking, he said that after he got let go by the Twins, the Tigers picked him up and converted him into a pitcher. He said that he pitched only one inning in his career and got the win, coming in relief in a game that Jack Morris

Box score
Second game

WINTER HAVEN	ab	r	h	bi	LAKELAND	ab	r	h	bi
Leach lf	4	0	0	0	Cabrra rf	4	1	1	0
Delgado ss	4	1	1	0	Galindo ss	4	1	2	1
Bagwll 3b	3	1	1	0	Pegues cf	4	1	2	1
Dgfico 1b	2	1	2	0	Spann lf	3	1	2	1
Whthad ph	1	0	1	0	Brogna 1b	2	0	0	0
Zmbrano rf	3	2	2	4	Hndrsn 1b	2	0	0	0
Tatum dh	4	0	1	0	Beyeler 2b	4	1	2	1
Laseke 2b	3	0	0	0	Mrigny 3b	3	1	2	1
Fagnant c	3	1	2	2	Baxter c	3	1	1	0
Rivers cf	3	0	1	0	Strong dh	1	0	0	0
					Hare ph	1	0	0	0
Totals	30	6	11	6	Totals	31	7	12	5

Winter Haven 014 001 0—6
Lakeland 000 031 3—7
Two out when winning run scored.
E—Wacha, Rivers, Zambrano. LOB— Winter Haven 6, Lakeland 6. DP— Winter Haven 2. 2B— Fagnant, Bagwill. 3B— Marigny. HR— Zambrano, Fagnant. SF— Spann.

	IP	H	R	ER	BB	SO
Winter Haven						
Landry	4.1	7	3	3	3	1
Wacha(L4-6)	2.1	5	4	1	0	1
Lakeland						
Morris	2	3	1	0	0	0
Willis	3	6	4	4	2	1
Kieley	1	1	1	0	0	0
Mrhrdt (W)	1	1	0	0	1	1

A—838.Stange. B—Simon. T— 2:43. A — 286.

started against Winter Haven. He said that Jeff Bagwell was on that team. He came in, threw a couple of pitches and got a broken bat two-hopper to short.

I said, "Greg, small world. I was the guy that hit the two-hopper to shortstop." I showed him the box score the next time I saw him.

It was the most bizarre season. One night, I was playing slow-pitch softball for Cigna Insurance and the next night, I was in the lineup in a Double-A game for New Britain. Then, a few weeks later, I was going hard off of Jack Morris and making an out against a guy that turned out to be a good friend twelve years later.

Darren Dreifort

Major League Clubs/Minor League Organizations:
LOS ANGELES DODGERS

Position: PITCHER

Team: SAN ANTONIO, TX

League: TEXAS

Year: 1994

DARREN DREIFORT was the eighteenth player in Major League base-ball history to reach the big leagues without first having any Minor League experience. The second overall selection behind Alex Rodriguez in the 1993 June draft, Dreifort pitched in 27 games with the Dodgers in 1994. Bothered by injuries his entire career, his best season came in 2000, when he posted a 12–9 mark with 164 strikeouts.

Dreifort played less than one season in the Minor Leagues in 1994. His memorable Minor League experience occurred while playing Class AA ball in the Los Angeles Dodgers organization.

I was playing in San Antonio for the Missions, and the mascot there was a guy named Puffy Taco.

One of the things that he would do was race a kid around the bases. He would start at first base while the kid would start at home plate. The taco guy would run around the bases and the kid would have to catch him.

But, they would get these big kids there who would absolutely pummel Puffy Taco. The kids could catch him about halfway home, and then they would basically pile-drive him.

Puffy Taco was not a very big guy. He would be running along and all of sudden, the kid would just pounce on him. It happened every night. He would keep coming out and would keep taking a beating. It was also the same guy in Puffy Taco every night.

It was one of the funniest things I had seen.

Brandon Webb

Major League Clubs/Minor League Organizations:
ARIZONA DIAMONDBACKS

Position: PITCHER

Team: EL PASO, TX

League: TEXAS

Year: 2000

BRANDON WEBB has established himself as a very durable big league pitcher. In 2004, he led the National League in games-started with 35, recorded 208 innings pitched, and had a respectable 3.59 ERA on a club that struggled scoring runs. In his rookie season with the Arizona Diamondbacks in 2003, he earned 10 victories and commanded a 2.84 ERA with 172 strikeouts.

Webb played parts of four seasons in the Minor Leagues from 2000 to 2003. His memorable Minor League experience occurred while playing Class AA ball in the Arizona Diamondbacks organization.

It was 2002 in El Paso.

Me and a couple of other guys had to do a community appearance at a zoo by the old Diablo Stadium. It was an old, bootleg zoo and just terrible.

There were probably one hundred kids there. I'm not really sure what the event was for. Well, they had us march and guide everyone around, holding this big banner marching to a kid song. We were chanting!

Then, we had to get up and hand something out on stage.

It was funny that we had to do all that because we didn't think that we would have to do anything.

Josh Beckett

Major League Clubs/Minor League
Organizations: FLORIDA MARLINS

Position: PITCHER

Team: PORTLAND, ME/BREVARD
COUNTY, FL

League: EASTERN/FLORIDA STATE

Year: 2001/2000

JOSH BECKETT was named the 2003
World Series Most Valuable Player at
just twenty-three years old, leading the
Florida Marlins to the championship over the New York Yankees in six
games. Beckett fired a complete game, two-hit shutout in the clincher at
Yankee Stadium and allowed just two runs on eight hits in 16.2 World
Series innings. In his first three seasons, the first overall pick in the 1999
June draft pitched 273 innings and recorded 289 strikeouts with a 3.33 ERA.

Beckett played parts of two seasons in the Minor Leagues from 2000
to 2001. His memorable Minor League experience occurred while playing Class A and AA ball in the Florida Marlins organization.

When I was in Double-A, I played in Portland, Maine. That
was the most unique city I ever played in because the
fans were like they are in Chicago with the Cubs.

They loved the Sea Dogs. That's what they do. The fans
would come out to the games and support that team. That was
such a big surprise to me, to be in a Minor League city and see
that.

But before I even got to Portland, I was in Brevard County.
That year was unbelievable and one of those special years where
when you go out for every start, your stuff's all good. I threw
39 straight scoreless innings that year. It was me and five other
guys staying in a house. All we did was stay up late to watch

movies, party, and have fun. We were also playing well and ended up winning that league.

We drew like seven people at every game. So, it wasn't like we were playing in front of big crowds. But, we played like a team. It was a lot like we did in Florida in 2003.

Randy Hennis was my pitching coach when I was in Brevard County. I was hurt the whole previous year and when I got with him, he had the balls to mess with me and get me back to where I was.

When I got drafted, I took a bunch of time off and didn't sign until late. Because I had a lot of time off, all it did was get me into bad habits or no habits at all.

He sat down with me and told me what we were going to focus on and do. That really helped me mechanically.

That's what I remember about the Minor Leagues.

John Flaherty

Major League Clubs/Minor League Organizations:
NEW YORK YANKEES, TAMPA BAY DEVIL RAYS,
BOSTON RED SOX, DETROIT TIGERS

Position: CATCHER

Team: ELMIRA, NY

League: NEW YORK-PENN

Year: 1988

JOHN FLAHERTY is a very well-liked and respected catcher in baseball. Throughout his thirteen-year Major League career, he has caught in over 1,000 games and served as both a proven starter and reliable backup in both leagues. His shining big league moment came in the bottom of the thirteenth inning at Yankee Stadium on July 1, 2004, against the Boston Red Sox, when his game-winning home run lifted the Yankees and ended the most epic regular-season battle between the bitter rivals.

Flaherty played parts of seven seasons in the Minor Leagues from 1988 to 1994. His memorable Minor League experience occurred while playing Class A ball in the Boston Red Sox organization.

My first memory of Minor League baseball was being sent to Elmira, New York, and not knowing what to expect.

I remember going on a road trip to Auburn to play the Astros, and we got $12 in meal money. It wasn't an overnight trip, so we basically had our uniforms on and went and played the game.

I thought the coolest thing was after the game, they sold us the hot dogs and hamburgers at a discounted price. I saved about $7 of my meal money and thought that it was a great deal back then.

I never had high expectations for the Minor Leagues, so I was never disappointed with the facilities or anything like that. I actually enjoyed it.

Randy Wolf

Major League Clubs/
Minor League Organizations:
PHILADELPHIA PHILLIES

Position: PITCHER

Team: BATAVIA, NY

League: NEW YORK-PENN

Year: 1997

RANDY WOLF has been a key member of the Philadelphia Phillies starting rotation since 1999. In his first five seasons, he collected 55 victories and struck out at least 150 batters in each of those years. An All-Star selection in 2003, he posted his best season yet by winning 16 games and fanning 177 batters.

Wolf played parts of three seasons in the Minor Leagues from 1997 to 1999. His memorable Minor League experience occurred while playing Class A ball in the Philadelphia Phillies organization.

I feel kind of bad telling this story, but I have to.

My first year was in Batavia in 1997. In Batavia, you lived with a host family that they set up for you. The house was right across from the ballpark, and the family was really nice.

But, they put me in the basement and in the basement, I slept on a mattress. It was not a bed, just a mattress, on the worst smelling carpet ever. I think they had a dog, and the dog used that as a litter box.

I remember thinking that I had to take a picture of this. So, I took pictures of the basement and where I was sleeping.

When you sign, and you go out to play ball, you think that it's going to be great right away. No. Not at all.

The smell was so bad. It was so bad. I really feel bad telling the story because the people were so nice. I just didn't have the heart to tell them that they really needed to change the carpet.

But I actually had a great time. It was the first time that I played pro ball and the first time I played with wood bats. I was just excited to be there.

So, the fact that I was sleeping on the smelly rug, I didn't really worry about it.

Bob Stanley

Major League Clubs/Minor League Organizations: BOSTON RED SOX
Position: PITCHER
Team: WINTER HAVEN, FL
League: FLORIDA STATE
Year: 1975

BOB STANLEY spent his entire thirteen-year Major League career with the Boston Red Sox. A native New Englander and both a starter and reliever, he was the first Red Sox pitcher in club history to record 100 wins and 100 saves in a career and is the all-time leader in appearances with 637.

Stanley played four seasons in the Minor Leagues from 1973 to 1976. His memorable Minor League experience occurred while playing Class A ball in the Boston Red Sox organization.

It was 1975 in the Florida State League. I was playing for Winter Haven, and our stadium lights were really bad. We were playing the Tampa Tarpons, which was the Cincinnati Reds team.

I was on the mound, and all of a sudden, the leadoff hitter comes up and he's got a flashlight taped to his helmet because our lights were so bad. He stepped in the box, then he stepped out, and then he turned the flashlight on.

I didn't know what to do. I started saying, "I can't pitch to this guy like this."

It ended up that the umpire kicked him out of the game, so I never had to face him. That would have been a first.

Chris Woodward

Major League Clubs/Minor League
Organizations: TORONTO BLUE JAYS

Position: SHORTSTOP

Team: MEDICINE HAT, ALBERTA,
CANADA

League: PIONEER

Year: 1995

CHRIS WOODWARD reached the Major
Leagues in 1999 with Toronto despite being
a 54th round pick in the 1995 June draft. A versatile athlete that has played
every infield position for the Blue Jays, he had a career year in 2002 by hitting 13 home runs and collecting 45 RBI. On August 7 versus Seattle that
season, he became the first Blue Jays shortstop in team history to hit three
home runs in one game.

Woodward played parts of eight seasons in the Minor Leagues from
1995 to 2001. His memorable Minor League experience occurred while
playing Class A ball in the Toronto Blue Jays organization.

There was one place that I just despised going to in the
Minor Leagues.

Fayetteville, North Carolina, was the worst ballpark that I
ever played in before they re-built it. There was no hitter's
background. The infield was the worst I ever played on, and by
the second inning, it was chewed up and hard as a rock.

There were no fans there except for some Marines, who came
from a local military base. These guys would sit along the top
deck of the stands and just get on you the whole game. They got
on me a few times. The first time they got in my head a bit, but
then I started to have some fun with them. They were so loud
that you could hear them from a few blocks away.

This place also had nothing open after the game. They never
had food in the clubhouse after the game except for some bread

and peanut butter, maybe. They had an orange juice machine that spat out pulp. I had to eat at a gas station one night because we went into extra innings and the only restaurant around closed at 9 P.M.

I got food poisoning after I decided to have two turkey sandwiches, which were probably wrapped up for about three weeks. I had to eat something because I didn't want to just eat candy bars for dinner. That whole night and the next day, I was throwing up. It was 110 degrees outside and miserable. Looking back on it now, I wonder how I got through it. It was what it was and I didn't know any different.

But any time that you can battle through that, it just makes you stronger. That was what weeded the guys out. Many of the guys don't make it because they get tired of that and think they are so far off. Mentally, they can't take it anymore so they don't put everything into it.

I think the Minor Leagues were a lot like the movie *Bull Durham*. The way the guys were with each other and the stupid little things they did to pass time. You didn't eat at fancy restaurants, you ate at Waffle House.

Gary Carter

Major League Clubs/Minor League Organizations: MONTREAL EXPOS, NEW YORK METS, SAN FRANCISCO GIANTS, LOS ANGELES DODGERS
Position: CATCHER
Team: JAMESTOWN, NY
League: NEW YORK-PENN
Year: 1972

GARY CARTER redefined the position of catcher in the 1970s and '80s. The eleven-time All-Star and two-time All-Star Game Most Valuable Player finished his career with 324 home runs, 1,225 RBI, and 2,056 games caught. The catalyst of the 1986 World Champion New York

Mets, "The Kid" was inducted into the National Baseball Hall of Fame in Cooperstown, New York, in 2003.

Carter played three seasons in the Minor Leagues from 1972 to 1974. His memorable Minor League experience occurred while playing Class A, AA, and AAA ball in the Montreal Expos organization.

Well, actually, there were so many memories from the Minor Leagues.

Just to begin things, when I first signed, I went to Jamestown, New York, to a tryout camp for two weeks. I didn't really know what to expect. Here, I had just signed and was all excited. It was 1972 and I was the Expos number-three pick, yet I really wasn't a catcher.

I was more of an infielder and played shortstop, third, first, and pitched a little bit. I would say that I really wasn't a polished catcher by any means. So, to start things off, we went there to really determine who was going to go where.

The number-one pick that year was Bobby Goodman, who was a catcher. He went out to play in Jamestown, which was the higher rookie club. The East Coast Gulf League was the lower rookie club, and I was designated to go to Cocoa Beach, Florida.

Ironically, that turned out to be a blessing because I proved myself within a month's time and was called up to West Palm Beach.

I didn't know what to expect when I got to Jamestown for this tryout thing. I had some good coaches who worked with me. I remember a guy by the name of Rick Summers, also Walt Hriniak was there, and then there was Bill McKenzie. They worked with me, and I started learning some of the fundamentals and art of catching. I got the opportunity in the Minor Leagues in Cocoa Beach, Florida, of catching on an everyday basis, and then I got called up to the Florida State League.

At that time, that was my biggest memory because I felt like we had no fans who watched us throughout that whole time in

Cocoa Beach. The only fans who came to the games were mostly parents of some of the players, and that was maybe a handful of people. I don't remember any crowds over ten. When I got called up to West Palm Beach, all of a sudden, they were starting to draw 1,000, 1,500, maybe 2,000 a night. I said, "This is what it's all about. This is professional baseball." I felt like I reached the big leagues at that point.

The following spring, I was invited to big league spring training camp because they always need an excess of catchers to catch all the pitchers. It was such a thrill to have just been out of high school at eighteen years old and go to big league spring training camp. I was so honored to have been invited.

Maybe because of my overzealous enthusiasm, it was Carl Kiehl who fought for me, the lesser round draft choice, instead of Bobby Goodman, to go to Double-A. I had a good double-A year. What I remember most about that season in Quebec City was being asked to be a part of the All-Star Game at Three Rivers. It was the biggest crowd I had played in front of at that point in my short career. I ended up being the MVP of the game and hit two home runs while going 4-for-4.

I think that may be what excited me every time I was honored to go to the Major League All-Star Game. I ended being the MVP of two All-Star Games in '81 and '84, and I always thought that was the time to prove what kind of player you really were.

When I got to Triple-A in Memphis the next year, we dominated the division and won it by over 20 games. We played against the Rochester Red Wings in the playoffs and turned out losing to them in a best-of-five series. But in the first game that we played, I was so fired up about making it to the playoffs that I hit two home runs, and we won 6–5. I had all six RBI. The headline in the paper the next day read, "Carter 6, Red Wings 5."

We had such a good team and were picked to win. We won the first two games and were coming home but ended up losing three straight, and Rochester won the International League that year. It was exciting for those kinds of things to happen to me in an early stage of my career.

Those were the biggest things that I remember. Not having any fans at the first place I was at to at least one thousand fans in West Palm Beach. The Double-A All-Star Game in 1973 was a thrill as was the playoffs in 1974.

I hate to pick out just one memory because there were so many great ones.

Paul Konerko

Major League Clubs/Minor League
Organizations: LOS ANGELES
DODGERS, CHICAGO WHITE SOX

Position: FIRST BASE

Team: ALBUQUERQUE, NM/
SAN ANTONIO, TX

League: PACIFIC COAST/TEXAS

Year: 1997

PAUL KONERKO is one of the best first basemen in the American League. Since joining the White Sox in 1999, he has averaged a .280 batting clip with 27 home runs and 94 RBI per season. The 2002 All-Star selection, who was 2 for 2 with two doubles and two RBI in the historic game which ended in a 7–7 tie after eleven innings, batted .304 with 27 homers and 104 RBI in 151 games that year. In 2004, he posted a career high 41 home runs and 117 RBI.

Konerko played parts of five seasons in the Minor Leagues from 1994 to 1998. His memorable Minor League experience occurred while playing Class AA and AAA ball in the Los Angeles Dodgers organization.

I was lucky enough coming up to have good managers.

John Shelby, who is now the first-base coach of Los Angeles, was my Double-A manager. Ron Roenicke, who is the third-base coach for the Angels now, was my manager in A ball. Those were two big years where you begin to develop. Glenn Hoffman, who is a coach with the Dodgers, too, was my manager in Triple-A.

Those guys got me in a period where I was kind of raw and didn't really play the game right. Their job was to nip it in the bud and make sure that I was going in the right direction. I remember going through a rough time in Triple-A when I wasn't getting any hits and things were going bad. I popped up a ball and didn't run it out to first base. I jogged it out. Had the ball dropped, I probably would not have been standing on second base.

Well, Hoff called me in and told me that no matter what, don't give people a reason to say something bad about you. He said, "Don't ever let them see you not run a ball out. Don't ever let them see you play the game differently because you're doing bad instead of good. That could become a nail in your coffin. Always run the ball out hard. Always play the game with integrity." I still think of that today.

He taught me how to play the game hard. When you were on defense, you were on defense. When you were hitting, you were hitting. After you hit it, you were running. It was all separate from one another, regardless of what you had been doing. It was all about playing the game hard for what it was at that point. It could be catching a ground ball or it could be trying to score from second on a hit.

Ninety-five percent of all of the people in the Minor Leagues had the talent to make it to the big leagues. If they didn't, they wouldn't have been drafted or signed. So, it was about how you conducted yourself. How you learned how to play the game and the mental side of it that was going to put you in the big leagues.

There were tons of guys that had a lot of talent that never made it. Those guys may have never learned how to control their emotions, never ran out balls during bad streaks or played hard on defense when things weren't going their way. That was the stuff in the big leagues that the coaches noticed and the front office noticed. You really had to learn how to balance everything out.

It really was a game of failure because as a hitter, you were making a lot of outs a lot of the time. It was all about how you were going to bounce back from that.

Trot Nixon

Major League Clubs/Minor League Organizations:
BOSTON RED SOX

Position: OUTFIELDER

Team: SARASOTA, FL

League: FLORIDA STATE

Year: 1995

TROT NIXON is the most productive and beloved Red Sox right fielder since Dwight Evans. His two-run double in Game 4 of the 2004 World Series against the St. Louis Cardinals sealed the Red Sox 3–0 win to crown them champions for the first time in eighty-six years. In 2003, he had a career year by posting a .306 batting average with 28 home runs and 86 RBI while leading Boston to the pennant. Nixon has also hit one of the most dramatic home runs in Sox history, an eleventh-inning, game-winning blast in Game 3 of the American League Division Series against Oakland that year.

Nixon played parts of five seasons in the Minor Leagues from 1994 to 1998. His memorable Minor League experience occurred while playing Class A ball in the Boston Red Sox organization.

I was playing in Sarasota, Florida, in A ball, and we were playing the Twins. Torii Hunter was on that team and Al Newman was the manager.

In the Florida State League, it was so miserably hot during the day and the nights were steamy. You didn't see a lot of home runs down in the Florida State League. You might see a few guys hit 20 here and there.

The game got going on and I got one or two hits early in the game. I can't remember how many runs it was but I know that we tied it up at the end of nine. We went to extra innings and instead of going like 2-for-4 that game, I went 3-for-10 because we played seventeen innings.

In my last six at-bats, I went up there just trying to hit a home run. I was not a home run hitter, but I tried to do whatever I could and hopefully got a fastball. Instead of possibly sneaking in two or three more hits, I got one more in there.

There was one guy on our team who hadn't played the whole game and just sat beside the manager, Tommy Barrett. It was one of my teammates and good friends, Dan Collier. He was a monster of a man at 6'4", 235 pounds and strong with about 4 percent body fat.

He was from Alabama and one of those country boys that was just country strong. He wasn't playing but he kept saying in the thirteenth inning that he could win the game. We said to him, "Please do something."

In the seventeenth inning, he went over to the manager and said, "Hey, put me in this inning and I promise you that I will end it." I sat there and said to myself, "Let him play." I was supposed to go up to Double-A in Trenton the next day and was thinking about how I would have to get up at the crack of dawn.

It was already close to midnight. Finally, there were two outs and we had a man on when he came up to the plate. We all sat there thinking how he called his shot. Three pitches later, boom! Home run to left field. Game over.

We were in the third-base dugout and just went nuts. When you are in the third-base dugout, and the runner who is going to first base turns back to look at the dugout, it's pretty funny.

I think that most of the fans that came to the game that night, which was probably a couple hundred, had actually stayed until the end.

It was the greatest home run that I had ever seen in the Minor Leagues.

Eric Byrnes

Major League Clubs/Minor League
Organizations: OAKLAND ATHLETICS

Position: OUTFIELDER

Team: MODESTO, CA

League: CALIFORNIA

Year: 1999

ERIC BYRNES became a fan favorite in
Oakland when he entered the everyday
lineup in early 2003. With his hard-nosed
play and enthusiasm, Eric led the A's in triples and stolen bases in his rookie
season and posted a career year in 2004 with a .283 average, 20 home runs
and 73 RBI.

Byrnes played parts of five seasons in the Minor Leagues from 1998
to 2002. His memorable Minor League experience occurred while playing Class A ball in the Oakland Athletics organization.

W e were in Victorville, California, during a heat wave in
the middle of the summer.

We just played a day-night doubleheader against High
Desert and had a six-hour bus trip back to Modesto. At this time,
I was not a veteran in the Cal League, but I was in my second
season in the league.

One of the things that you like as a player in your second season in the same league is your own seat on the bus. It was 115
degrees outside, and the air conditioning was not working.

I was the last guy to get on the bus because I was outside saying goodbye to friends and family. When I did get on the bus,
there weren't any seats open. I was so pissed! I said, "You've got
to be kidding me," looking at guys who just got called up from
rookie ball that had their own seat on the bus.

So, because no one was going to move and I wanted to make a point, I stripped down buck-naked and stood in the aisle of the bus for the entire ride.

Six hours, buck-naked, during the whole bus trip from Victorville to Modesto.

Mike Neu

Major League Clubs/Minor League Organizations:
CINCINNATI REDS, OAKLAND ATHLETICS, FLORIDA MARLINS
Position: PITCHER
Team: CLINTON, IA
League: MIDWEST
Year: 1999

MIKE NEU broke into the Major Leagues on one of the best pitching staffs in baseball with Oakland in 2003. He earned his first big league save in a 17–2 rout over the Toronto Blue Jays, the same game that the Athletics set a club record by hitting two grand slams in one game.

Neu played parts of five seasons in the Minor Leagues from 1999 to 2004. His memorable Minor League experience occurred while playing Class A ball in the Cincinnati Reds organization.

You would think that my most memorable experience of the Minor Leagues would be something on the field, but for me it was far from it.

I grew up in the Bay Area in California and went to college at the University of Miami. My first full season in professional baseball was in Clinton, Iowa, which right off the bat was a lot different from what I was used to.

I lived in a two-bedroom place that was part of an apartment complex with four of my teammates. It was cheap and close to the ballpark. However, this was no ordinary complex, because it was actually an old mortuary. So, as you could imagine, it wasn't an ideal living environment.

Clinton was a real small town and home of a dog food manufacturing plant. It smelled really bad there all of the time. Anyone that has ever played in Clinton would tell you how bad it stunk. I literally had to put my shirt over my nose when I walked though town.

The people who lived in our apartment complex were not the same people that I was used to being around, either.

For example, there was one time where we had a bat flying throughout our apartment. The five of us were all freaking out, trying to hit the bat with a broom to get it into the hallway.

Finally, this guy who lived next door and was a Clinton native came out to see what was going on. I remember him as a very rough and ragged-looking guy. With the bat now flying around the hallway, he went back into his apartment and returned with a small kit in hand.

As we stood there confused and watching him closely, he pulled out a blow dart gun and pointed it directly at the bat. After the bat landed and from about ten yards away, he shot the dart through the gun and immediately killed the bat.

I, absolutely amazed, stood there and said to myself, "Oh my god, where am I right now?"

Jeff Weaver

Major League Clubs/Minor League
Organizations: DETROIT TIGERS,
NEW YORK YANKEES, LOS ANGELES
DODGERS

Position: PITCHER

Team: COMSTOCK PARK, MI

League: MIDWEST

Year: 1998

JEFF WEAVER reached the big leagues after only six Minor League starts in the Detroit Tigers organization. In four seasons with the Tigers, he won 39 games before being traded to the New York Yankees in July of 2002. Traded for Kevin Brown before the 2004 season, Weaver had his best year yet by going 13–13 with a 4.01 ERA in 34 starts for the Los Angeles Dodgers.

Weaver played parts of two seasons in the Minor Leagues from 1998 to 1999. His memorable Minor League experience occurred while playing Class A and AA ball in the Detroit Tigers organization.

I was in short-season Jamestown and only had two starts when I got sent to pitch in West Michigan for the White Caps in the postseason. I had three starts in the postseason and we ended up winning the championship.

That was my first summer of pro ball and that was my first championship. It was a real fun experience, and you start to think that everything will go your way.

I had one start in Double-A the next year before I went up, so I only had six starts in the minors.

But, my first fifteen-hour bus ride was a real experience for me. It grounded me really quick. Stopping at McDonald's with the $5 of meal money that I'd get was pretty crazy. I remember getting on the bus when everybody already had their own seat and thinking, "What's going on here."

They definitely don't make buses for anybody over 6'5". Your back would be all jacked up and you would be squirming around just trying to find a comfortable position.

I was very glad to put that all behind me and get to where the fun really begins, and where you travel by plane.

Latroy Hawkins

Major League Clubs/Minor League Organizations:
MINNESOTA TWINS, CHICAGO CUBS

Position: PITCHER

Team: SALT LAKE CITY, UT

League: PACIFIC COAST

Year: 1995

LATROY HAWKINS has established himself as a strong late-game pitcher after beginning his career as a starter. In 2004, he saved 25 games as the closer for the Cubs after originally signing to be the set-up man. With the Twins from 2000–03, Hawkins posted 42 saves over two seasons as a closer and a 15–3 record with a 2.00 ERA and 138 strikeouts in two seasons as a set-up man.

Hawkins played parts of seven seasons in the Minor Leagues from 1991 to 1997. His memorable Minor League experience occurred while playing Class AAA ball in the Minnesota Twins organization.

I made the team out of spring training right after the strike, so we only had a few weeks to get ready. I made the team because they expanded the rosters then, but I got sent back down as soon as they put the rosters back to 25.

During that All-Star break, I was in Salt Lake City in Triple-A and hating baseball. I was really hating it and said to myself, "I think I'm going to quit."

I went home to Gary, Indiana, during the All-Star break and thought that maybe I'll come back and maybe I won't. I didn't tell anybody at home, nobody, about what I was thinking. When

I got home, I saw guys that I played high school baseball, basketball, and ran track with. They were asking me for two dollars. They'd say, "Let me get a couple dollars, man."

Reality set in right then and there. I knew that baseball was what I wanted to do, and that I was going to put my heart, my soul, and my all into it. When I got back to Salt Lake City, I told my pitching coach Rick Anderson that I thought about not coming back. He said, "What?" He was glad that I did come back.

I saw how my friends were living, staying with their parents and stuff, and thought to myself how I couldn't give up what I had. People would give up their right arm to get where I was. I was already at Triple-A, so I was already knocking at the door.

That's the one thing that I really remember about the Minor Leagues, how I went home during the All-Star break and had serious intentions of not coming back.

Gabe Kapler

Major League Clubs/Minor League Organizations:
DETROIT TIGERS, TEXAS RANGERS,
BOSTON RED SOX

Position: OUTFIELDER

Team: JACKSONVILLE, FL

League: SOUTHERN

Year: 1998

GABE KAPLER became an immediate fan favorite in Boston after just his first week on the job at Fenway Park in 2003. In his first two games as a member of the Red Sox, he went 7-for-9 with two home runs and seven RBI. Kapler, who established himself as a dynamic outfielder with power and speed with Detroit and Texas, totaled 51 home runs and 53 stolen bases in his first four Major League seasons. Before reaching the big leagues with the Tigers in 1998, he batted .322 with 28 home runs and 146 RBI in 139 games for Jacksonville.

Kapler played parts of eight seasons in the Minor Leagues from 1995 to 2003. His memorable Minor League experience occurred while playing Class A ball in the Detroit Tigers organization.

There were so many special moments from Minor League baseball for me. I loved my experience in the Minor Leagues. It was very difficult, but at the same time, it was so rewarding.

I didn't pay too much attention to stuff that I did on the field. I kept a couple of balls for my dad from record hits or record doubles, but when I was involved in a season, I didn't ever realize how good of a year I was having. It wasn't until I went home in the off-season that I would think about the special parts of the season.

My wife, Lisa, came with me everywhere that I went. She was very supportive and I would not have been able to get through that part of my life without her, no doubt about it.

I was not the kind of guy who was constantly going out and drinking. If I was, I don't think I would have been a very good baseball player. I put in a lot of time and effort off of the field to make myself a productive baseball player. The only way I knew how to do that was to work really hard. Lisa was very supportive of that fact. I would always go and train everywhere that I went on the road and at home. My wife made that possible for me.

I knew some guys whose wives paid attention to what went on on the field. That can be somewhat overwhelming. I heard stories of guys who had bad games, went home, and had their wives or significant others grill them as to what went on in the game and why X, Y, and Z happened.

For me, it was the complete opposite, which was always a blessing. I never came home and had my wife ask me why I struggled. My wife was amazing. She didn't care about what went on in the game, and I liked that. That helped me.

Geoff Jenkins

Major League Clubs/Minor League Organizations:
MILWAUKEE BREWERS
Position: OUTFIELD
Team: EL PASO, TX
League: TEXAS
Year: 1996

GEOFF JENKINS may play in a small market but he carries a big bat. In his six full big league seasons with the Milwaukee Brewers, he has averaged over 23 home runs and 76 RBI. Jenkins posted consecutive 25-plus home run and 90-plus RBI seasons in 2003 and 2004, earning a trip to the All-Star Game in 2003. He had his most productive season in 2000, when he batted .303 with 34 homers and 94 RBI.

Jenkins played parts of four seasons in the Minor Leagues from 1995 to 1998. His memorable Minor League experience occurred while playing Class AA ball in the Milwaukee Brewers organization.

I was playing in Double-A with El Paso in 1996.

You weren't making too much money and so you had to go wherever you could to eat and stuff. Whoever got the Player of the Game would get these certificates that you were the Wonderburger What A Player of the Game.

So, whoever won this best-player-of-the-game would take the other guys to eat. Every third day, my roommate or I would win these certificates. We would take each other and feed each other there for basically the whole season.

Back then, you were younger and could eat whatever you wanted. It was pretty funny.

Alex Cora

Major League Clubs/Minor League
Organizations: LOS ANGELES DODGERS

Position: SHORTSTOP

Team: SAN ANTONIO, TX

League: TEXAS

Year: 1997

ALEX CORA may be the most unheralded
middle infielder in baseball. Since 2001, he
has averaged over 125 games played between second base and shortstop
for the Dodgers. In 2004, he posted a .987 fielding percentage after com-
mitting just eight errors in nearly 1,100 innings played. In addition, he set
career highs for home runs with 10 and RBI with 47.

Cora played parts of five seasons in the Minor Leagues from 1996 to
2000. His memorable Minor League experience occurred while playing
Class AA ball in the Los Angeles Dodgers organization.

I was drafted out of the University of Miami, and I got pretty
lucky because I got to play in the Florida State League, which
was really not that bad.

The next year in 1997, I went to Double-A in San Antonio.
Tommy Lasorda came in because they wanted him to work with
me in batting practice.

It was the middle of July, and it was so hot and humid. He's
there giving me advice, telling me to start chopping wood and
to snap my hips. Well, we get to the game and I hit four fly balls.

He came over and I asked him right away, "What did I do
wrong?" He said, "You hit four fly balls. If you want to make
money in the big leagues, you better start hitting the ball on the
ground."

Julio Mosquera

Major League Clubs/Minor League Organizations:
TORONTO BLUE JAYS, TAMPA BAY DEVIL RAYS,
NEW YORK YANKEES, TEXAS RANGERS,
SEATTLE MARINERS
Position: CATCHER
Team: SYRACUSE, NY
League: INTERNATIONAL
Year: 1996

JULIO MOSQUERA is a student of the game and modern-day "Crash Davis." His drive, insight, and experience have kept him attractive to teams in need of a veteran catcher in their Minor League system. He reached the Major Leagues with the Toronto Blue Jays in 1996 and collected seven hits in 30 at-bats over two seasons. In 1,015 Minor League games, he has a career average of .281 with 50 home runs and 433 RBI.

Mosquera has played parts of fourteen seasons in the Minor Leagues from 1991 to 2004. His memorable Minor League experience occurred while playing Class AAA ball in the Toronto Blue Jays organization.

My most memorable Minor League story was in Syracuse, New York, in 1996 while I was playing in Triple-A for the Syracuse Sky Chiefs.

My manager was Richie Hebner, and I was staying in the hotel because I just got called up from Double-A. It was around 5:30 A.M., and Richie came over and started banging on the door.

My roommate at the time was Rickey Cradle, an outfielder who also just got called up to Triple-A. We were there for only about two weeks. When I heard the banging on the door, I thought to myself, "What the hell is going on here?"

Honestly, I was a little scared because it was so early in the morning and I didn't know who it was. So, I told my roommate to get up and open the door. He told me that I should get up.

Well, he got up and it was Richie. He came in like he was pissed off and said, "Where's Julio?" I said, "I'm here." He said,

"Get up! What are you doing?" I told him that I was sleeping because it was early in the morning.

He told me to get my butt ready and that I probably thought that I was dreaming. But, I needed to get ready because I was going to the big leagues! He said, "Your flight leaves at 9 A.M. You have to get ready so that you can go back to the field and get all your stuff. I will come back and pick you up in a half hour."

I didn't understand. I didn't know if I was dreaming. I didn't know what I was doing.

But, I got up right away and started packing up all of my stuff. I called my wife Jennifer and told her, "Guess what? I'm going to the big leagues." She couldn't believe it and was so happy. She started calling her mom and everybody.

I finished packing up but I didn't have a suit or anything. You didn't need that in the minors. But, in the big leagues, you had to dress nice. So, I just put on a long-sleeve shirt and some pants.

The Blue Jays were playing in Minnesota, which was real exciting for me because my hero growing up was Rod Carew, who began his career there.

I got to the stadium clubhouse and the first person I saw was the manager, Cito Gaston. He was there with a couple of the coaches. He said, "Julio, come here. Congratulations on making it to the big leagues."

I said, "Thank you, thank you."

Then, just to joke with me, he said, "You know that we have a dress code up here." He saw that I was little nervous and I told him that I wasn't really expecting this. He told me not to worry about it and to go with the team to get dressed and stretched.

I couldn't believe it. I made it to the big leagues.

Keith Foulke

Major League Clubs/Minor League
Organizations: SAN FRANCISCO,
CHICAGO WHITE SOX, OAKLAND
ATHLETICS, BOSTON RED SOX

Position: PITCHER

Team: EVERETT, WA

League: NORTHWEST

Year: 1994

KEITH FOULKE pitched his way into Boston fame and baseball history
with his dominating performances over the St. Louis Cardinals in the
2004 World Series and the New York Yankees in the American League
Championship Series. Appearing in all four World Series games, he was
1–0 with one save and a 1.80 ERA over five innings. In Game 4, his grab
and toss to first base to record the final out gave Boston its first World
Series title in eighty-six years. Against the Yankees, Foulke appeared in five
of the seven games played and fired six scoreless innings to propel the Red
Sox to a history-making Series comeback victory.

Foulke played parts of four seasons in the Minor Leagues from 1994
to 1997. His memorable Minor League experience occurred while playing Class A ball in the San Francisco Giants organization.

The first place that I played after I signed was in Everett,
Washington. I can't really say that I envisioned a whole lot
about the minors because I thought that I was lucky to be drafted.

When they offered me money to sign and play professionally,
I was blown away. The ballparks were almost a step backwards
because the college league that I played in had some pretty nice
fields.

The furthest trip we had was to Boise, which was about
twelve hours or so. Maybe I just destroyed all of those memories, but that long on a bus trip was not fun. I would stare out
the window a lot and think about what I was going to do when
I got home.

The pay was very minimal. There were a lot of Taco Bells in there. When you were on the road, you would order a large pizza thinking that it was three days worth of meals. You would go put it on the air conditioner. I didn't really eat out a whole lot. The spreads at the field would be pizza after the game, maybe. You were pretty much limited to peanut butter and jelly after batting practice.

We lived with host families the first couple of years, and they did a good job taking care of us. That was a great experience, and I guess it showed that my parents did a good job raising me because I never got in any trouble or destroyed anything. I still keep in touch with a couple of them.

When we were in Seattle, my family from there came out. They took really good care of me and gave me a good spot to live. I was fortunate because I had good host parents.

My pitching coach in Short-A, Keith Comstock, was a big influence on me. I threw a forkball in college, and when I got there, the Giants said no more of that. He showed me the basics of how to throw a circle change and I started throwing that.

I went down that year with shoulder problems. I only pitched in a couple of games but worked on that over the next few years. In 1999, when I was with the White Sox, that pitch kind of came out.

Everyone would go through times that you thought you wouldn't make it to the Major Leagues. You'd go through a little rough streak and question yourself if you were good enough to play at the next level.

I was lucky because I had success at every level and kept moving up. Fortunately, the front office also liked me.

Luis Sojo

Major League Clubs/Minor League Organizations:
NEW YORK YANKEES, TORONTO BLUE JAYS,
CALIFORNIA ANGELS, SEATTLE MARINERS,
PITTSBURGH PIRATES
Position: INFIELDER/THIRD-BASE COACH
Team: MYRTLE BEACH, SC
League: SOUTH ATLANTIC
Year: 1987

LUIS SOJO may be best remembered for driving in the 2000 World Series clinching run for the New York Yankees with a ninth-inning single off of Al Leiter in Game 5 against the New York Mets at Shea Stadium. In his six seasons played with the Yankees, he won four World Series titles in 1996, 1998, 1999, and 2000. In 2002, Luis managed the Yankees Double-A club in Norwich, Connecticut, to the Eastern League Championship. Prior to the 2004 season, he was named the Yankees third base coach.

Sojo played parts of eight seasons in the Minor Leagues from 1987 to 1995. His memorable Minor League experience occurred while playing Class A ball in the Toronto Blue Jays organization.

For some reason, there was a nice old couple that loved me. In Myrtle Beach, you had to walk through the fans before the game started to get on the field. One day, this couple stopped me and told me that I was going to have a good game today. I didn't know what they said because I didn't speak any English. So, I just nodded my head and said, "Thank you, thank you."

About one month after the season started, I saw the old man again. He stopped a friend of mine from Venezuela who spoke English and gave him $20. He said, "Make sure you give this to Luis. Tell him to take it and have a nice steak."

I was so skinny.

I took the money and after the game, I made sure to go out to a nice steak place and had a steak. Every few days, he would give me another $20 because he wanted me to keep eating steaks.

Then, this old couple found out where I lived. They were nice, retired people with nothing to do. So, they came to my apartment, which I only paid $75 per month for, and opened my refrigerator. There was nothing in there except for water. They said, "When you ever need anything, you let us know."

They were talking to me but I didn't know what they were saying. So, I had to grab my friend to tell me what they said.

The only thing I needed was to go to the supermarket. It was pretty far away and I didn't have a driver's license. So, they started taking me to the supermarket every Friday, and by the time I got to the register, they had already paid. They wouldn't let me pay for anything.

I really appreciated what they did for me. They were really nice people. It was hard to keep in touch with them after the season because I didn't speak English.

I went back there the next year and they really took care of me again. I learned a little bit of English and was able to communicate with them. They were good people.

When people show you love, you realize that you belong here in the United States. You know that you are going to spend a lot of years over here, and so when you find people who care for you, that's when you realize that you can make it here for a long time.

Drew Henson

Major League Clubs/Minor League Organizations:
NEW YORK YANKEES, CINCINNATI REDS

Position: THIRD BASE

Team: MARYVALE, AZ

League: ARIZONA FALL

Year: 2001

DREW HENSON reached the Major Leagues in 2002 after foregoing his senior season of college football eligibility as quarterback at the University of Michigan in 2001. Drafted by the Houston Texans in April of 2003, he left baseball in early 2004 and was traded to the Dallas Cowboys.

Henson played parts of six seasons in the Minor Leagues from 1998 to 2003. His memorable Minor League experience occurred while playing Arizona Fall League ball in the New York Yankees organization.

It was the fall of 2001, and Nick Johnson and I were hanging out with some of my friends from home at my apartment in Arizona during the Fall League. It was late one night, and I let one of my buddies take my truck down to the gas station to pick up some subs. He had my cell phone so that he could call and get our orders when he got there.

He called about fifteen minutes later, and I thought that he was going to ask me what I wanted on my sandwich. Instead, he told me my car was stolen. I didn't believe him, of course, because why would he bring my cell phone inside with him but forget my keys. For some reason, he left the keys on the floor of the car.

Someone must have stuck his head in, grabbed them and took off. My car was gone. I had to jump in another ride, go down to the police station around 2 A.M., talk to the police, fill out the police report, and not know if I would ever see my truck again.

It was Scottsdale, of all places, so you think it's a nice area, but it could happen anywhere. The police wound up finding it the next day. Two eighteen-year-old kids had taken it down to Tempe and were blaring my bass while driving around a mall parking lot. A policeman told them to slow down, ran the plates, and found out it was my car.

I ended up getting it back, but they took everything out of it including my CDs, DVDs, and stereo. So now I don't let other people drive my car at night anymore.

Scott Chaisson

Major League Clubs/Minor League Organizations:
CHICAGO CUBS, OAKLAND ATHLETICS,
KANSAS CITY ROYALS
Position: PITCHER
Team: HAINES CITY, FL
League: SPRING TRAINING
Year: 1998

SCOTT CHAISSON was drafted in the fifth round of the June 1998 draft by the Kansas City Royals. Considered to be one of the top college players to come out of the state of Connecticut in more than ten years, he was the focal prospect in two trades in his first four professional seasons and is still striving to reach the Major Leagues.

Chaisson has played seven seasons in the Minor Leagues from 1998 to 2004. His memorable Minor League experience occurred while playing Class A ball in the Kansas City Royals organization.

We were in spring training during my first year of pro ball in Haines City, Florida. I was with the Kansas City Royals, where they had dorms for the players. The younger players had to stay in their dorms. It was two to a bunk bed, with a high bunk and a low bunk.

My roommate and I, who was a first-rounder with the Royals and a young kid, would have to be in by 11 P.M. The doors of the dorm would get locked every night at 11 P.M., and that's it. If you weren't in the dorm by eleven o'clock, you couldn't get in.

The whole spring training that year, my roommate and I would take turns going out to the bars and stay there until 1 or 2 A.M. When we got back, we obviously couldn't get in. Most of the time, we would prop open a door somehow and get back into the dorm.

Well, one night we all went out and came back unable to get in. No one was getting in! We were stuck outside, so we had no choice but to sleep in our trucks that night. It was fine, because somebody woke up early and got everyone else up.

I then decided that I wasn't going to stay in the damn dorms anymore, and chose to sleep in my truck for the rest of spring training. I would put a note on my roommate's car that I was in my truck sleeping. At 6 A.M. every morning, he would shake my truck, wake me up, and we would go to the field.

No one ever found out. I actually had a pretty good spring training and ended up getting traded to Oakland as the player to be named later for Jay Witasick. I went to Oakland, and that's when my professional career really got started.

Pat Hentgen

Major League Clubs/Minor League
Organizations: TORONTO BLUE JAYS,
ST. LOUIS CARDINALS, BALTIMORE
ORIOLES

Position: PITCHER

Team: ST. CATHARINES, ONTARIO,
CANADA

League: NEW YORK-PENN

Year: 1986

PAT HENTGEN was one of the best pitchers of the 1990s. Over his fourteen-year Major League career, he started 304 games, fired 2,075 innings, won 131 games, and recorded 1,290 strikeouts. In 1996, he won the American League Cy Young Award with a 20–10 record and a 3.22 ERA. The three-time All-Star was the Game 3 winning pitcher in the Blue Jays 1993 World Series Championship over Philadelphia.

Hentgen played parts of six seasons in the Minor Leagues from 1986 to 1992. His memorable Minor League experience occurred while playing Class A ball in the Toronto Blue Jays organization.

I was in St. Catharines, Ontario and seventeen years old. When the games ended, I didn't even know how to get home. We stayed in a nursing dorm next to a hospital, and that was where nurses used to live.

When the season started, it was just an empty building with all players on our floor. Everybody had their own little cubicle, sink, and shared the showers and bathrooms. I was right out of high school and remember thinking after the games, "How do I get home? Was there a bus?"

No. You were on your own. I had never even been in a taxi-cab my whole life, as I grew up just an hour outside of Detroit. There was never a need to have a cab. I remember calling my parents and having them bring my car up. I was one of three guys on the team that actually had a car because I only lived four hours from St. Catherines.

I remember asking one of our pitchers, Bob Cavanaugh, "Do you want to ride with me?" He looked me right in the eyes and said, "I'm not getting in the car with you. You just got your license less than a year ago." He was a college guy.

I played five and a half years in the Minor Leagues and hit every level. There were some levels that I hit twice. I was shocked with how good everybody was. Coming from a small high school just outside of Detroit, I was probably the best player on the team. I couldn't believe how much talent there was, and the guys out of college were three or four years older than me. Everybody was a lot stronger, bigger. I was overwhelmed with how everyone was 6'2", 200 pounds.

I made the All-Star team in 1987 but when I started the year in Dunedin in 1988, I began the year 0–9 and finished the year at 3–12. I definitely had a lot of self-doubt and looking back, I was only nineteen. I always competed against guys that were a lot older than me but never realized that I was young and naive.

They used to tell us that if you could get to Double-A, that was the hardest jump—from A ball to Double-A. After going through the Minor Leagues, I never thought that was the hardest jump. I thought that the hardest jump was from Triple-A to the big leagues.

John Schiffner

Major League Clubs/Minor League Organizations:
PITTSBURGH PIRATES

Position: CATCHER

Team: BRADENTON, FL

League: SPRING TRAINING

Year: 1978

JOHN SCHIFFNER never reached the Major Leagues, but he has certainly made a name for himself in baseball as one of the most successful managers in the history of the prestigious Cape Cod League. In twelve seasons as skipper of the Chatham A's, he has compiled over 260 wins and two League Championships as well as managing over 500 games. In 2001, famed actor Brian Dennehy portrayed Schiffner in the movie *Summer Catch*, which starred Freddie Prinze, Jr. and story-lined Cape Cod League baseball.

Schiffner played one season in the Minor Leagues in 1978. His memorable Minor League experience occurred while playing Class A ball in the Pittsburgh Pirates organization.

It was very late in Major League spring training but very early in Minor League spring training camp.

All of the rookie league and Class A guys would come in much later than the Major League guys then. A bunch of guys, some back from the year before and others as new signees, were in camp in mid-March. The Major League and Minor League spring training sites were side-by-side at Pirate City, and Bradenton was a pretty small city.

After a few days of hanging around camp, we decided that we were going to go out and test the town out. So, we went into a spot that looked pretty nice and had a couple of beers. It was one of our first afternoons off and there were about five or six of us just sitting around talking baseball.

All of a sudden, in came the Pirates. Willie Stargell, Manny Sanguillen, Phil Garner, and the like. I remember thinking, "Oh god, I think we've chosen a bad spot, boys." They recognized us but nothing was said.

After about a half hour went by, we got more apprehensive and nervous that we might be in the wrong place and in their spot. Then, we thought that all of our fears came true when Stargell stood up and started walking toward us. A million things were running through my mind, as this was Willie Stargell walking toward me.

He came over and just said, "Hey fellas. I recognize you guys from camp and want to wish you the best of luck. I hope that you all do real well." Then, he slapped a $100 bill down on the table and said, "Drinks are on me. Enjoy yourselves and again, best of luck to all of you."

We couldn't believe it. Willie Stargell just bought us a drink. In fact, he bought us a lot of drinks because $100 went quite a ways in 1978.

Then, they all finished their sandwiches, gave us a wave and took off. It was so great and really neat. I think that definitely makes the legend of Stargell true because he really was a wonderful person.

I didn't need it to be proven to me, but that was just him. He was really great.

David Eckstein

Major League Clubs/Minor League
Organizations: BOSTON RED SOX,
ANAHEIM ANGELS

Position: SHORTSTOP

Team: SARASOTA, FL/TRENTON, NJ

League: FLORIDA STATE/EASTERN

Year: 1998

DAVID ECKSTEIN is Major League baseball's example of proving the
doubters wrong. At 5-8, 165 pounds, many believed that he was not big
enough, strong enough, or even good enough to be a big league player.
However, Eckstein has been just the opposite and a core member of the
Anaheim Angels. His best season came in 2002, when he batted .293 with
eight home runs, 63 RBI and 21 stolen bases to help lead the Angels to
their first-ever World Series title.

Eckstein played four seasons in the Minor Leagues from 1997 to 2000.
His memorable Minor League experience occurred while playing Class A
ball in the Boston Red Sox organization.

When I was in the Florida State League, we had a commuter trip for about a week.

We would jump on the bus from Sarasota and drive to
Tampa. The bus had no air conditioning, and we had one of those
old school buses with curtains on the windows.

Everyone was in their shorts and underwear because it was
so hot. We were just dead sweating on the bus. That was the way
we had to go to those games. It was pretty funny. The bus was
like a *Bull Durham*-type bus, and this was 1998.

I remember that we would watch movies like *Stripes* and
Field of Dreams. But, the movie had to be a good one, or the guy
who got the movie would get yelled at the whole time.

In order to pass the time on long trips after the game, I would
lay down on the floor under the seats and sleep. I was small

enough to fit underneath the seats. I would bring my heavy jacket, put it on the floor and sleep on that.

People liked sitting with me because they would get two seats to themselves.

Stump Merrill

Major League Clubs/Minor League Organizations:
PHILADELPHIA PHILLIES, NEW YORK YANKEES
Position: CATCHER/MANAGER
Team: EUGENE, OR
League: PACIFIC COAST LEAGUE
Year: 1970–1971

STUMP MERRILL managed two seasons in the Major League and twenty years in the minors with the New York Yankees. In 1990 and '91, Merrill led the Yankees to 120 victories and has also served as a Major League coach and front office advisor within the organization. He has compiled over 1,300 wins as a Minor League skipper.

Merrill played six seasons in the Minor Leagues from 1966 to 1971 and has managed since 1978. His memorable Minor League experience occurred while playing Class AAA ball in the Philadelphia Phillies organization.

I was playing for the Eugene Emeralds, who were the Triple-A club of the Philadelphia Phillies. It either was 1970 or 1971, and I can't even remember who we were playing. I should say Hawaii to make it look good because they were in the league, but I really can't remember.

I have told this story several times over the years, and in the old days, if I had a couple of social sparklers, I could animate along with it and it got to be a little better story.

But, actually, the fact of the matter of what happened was the count went to 3–2 on me, and then they had a bomb scare. We all had to evacuate the stadium. I think it was fifty-seven minutes later when I stepped back into the box and just knew damn well that he was going to throw me a fastball. He threw me a back-door breaking ball, and I took it for a called third strike.

It was the longest strikeout in the history of the game of baseball . . . fifty-seven minutes.

I don't remember who I was facing except for that he was right-handed. There was a comment in the paper the next day from me saying that, "It's a record that you really don't want to have, but it's probably one that will never be broken."

As a manager, there were a lot of stories that stick out about the Minor Leagues, but there aren't any that I would want in a book.

Gary Sheffield

Major League Clubs/Minor League
Organizations: MILWAUKEE BREWERS,
SAN DIEGO PADRES, FLORIDA MARLINS,
LOS ANGELES DODGERS,
ATLANTA BRAVES,
NEW YORK YANKEES

Position: OUTFIELD

Team: HELENA, MT

League: PIONEER

Year: 1986

GARY SHEFFIELD is one of the most productive offensive outfielders in Major League baseball. Over his seventeen-year career, he has a lifetime batting average of .298 with 362 home runs and 1,207 RBI. The eight-time All-Star had his best year in 2003 when he hit 39 home runs and collected 132 RBI for Atlanta. He won a World Series with the Florida Marlins in 1997, batting .292 with a home run and five RBI in seven games.

Sheffield played parts of four seasons in the Minor Leagues from 1986 to 1989. His memorable Minor League experience occurred while playing Class A ball in the Milwaukee Brewers organization.

My first year was in Helena, Montana, and I didn't know where it was. I was drafted by the Milwaukee Brewers and was thinking that I was going to Milwaukee. My flight said Helena, Montana, and I was like, "I was drafted by Milwaukee." The next thing I knew, I was landing in Helena and that is where my career got started.

I was in culture shock. I had never been past St. Petersburg, Florida, and Williamsport, Pennsylvania. Those were the only two places that I had ever traveled to. I had just gone on a recruiting trip at the University of Miami, where Greg Vaughn took me around.

That helped ease it a little bit because he got drafted by the Milwaukee Brewers, too. I knew somebody and I was comfortable with that. He showed me the ropes of how things go in the Minor Leagues.

I had seven roommates and my bed was at the front door. If somebody came in late and opened the front door, they would probably hit me in the face with the door. We didn't have a lot of money back then, living off $7 per day in meal money and having a rent of $400 per month. With seven roommates, you were able to afford more things and so you had a lot of pizza and beer.

When I was in A ball, I was the guy that everyone called a bonus baby. I was playing well but used to get fined for not wearing socks and a collared shirt while we were traveling. Being from Tampa, Florida, I never wore socks and a collared shirt.

I thought that I was being singled out because I saw other guys who didn't have on a collared shirt. The coach would just walk right by them, but tell me that I was fined $20 or $30. That was a big deal then because it was more than my meal money per day. I had to save up to be able to afford that.

It was a situation that was pretty hard. You would take crockpots on the road, trying to stretch a meal. But that was a defining moment for me because I went through the hard times then. It made me a better person as far as my character because I realized it was nothing personal that they were doing to hurt me.

It was to develop me into the guy who set the example for everyone else. It took me quite a while to understand that.

Todd Donovan

Major League Clubs/Minor League Organizations:
SAN DIEGO PADRES

Position: OUTFIELD

Team: PEORIA, AZ

League: SPRING TRAINING

Year: 2001

TODD DONOVAN was selected in the eighth round of the 1999 June draft by the San Diego Padres. Still striving to reach the Major Leagues, he has collected 164 stolen bases in six Minor League seasons and appeared in three spring training games between 2003 and 2004.

Donovan has played six seasons in the Minor Leagues from 1997 to 2003. His memorable Minor League experience occurred while playing Class A ball in the San Diego Padres organization.

I was a big Boston Red Sox fan growing up, but I went to school in Albany, New York. It was the year of the Subway Series, with New York against New York. Obviously, I am not a big Yankees fan.

I went out and bought a New York Mets hat. I wore it the entire time I was there, and then I left for spring training early to spend some time in San Diego. I had a little problem with my elbow, and I had to go to San Diego to see a doctor.

I was at a workout one day with my agent and a bunch of his clients, hanging out on the beach having a good time. Then, I got a phone call on my cell that the Padres needed to see me at Qualcomm Stadium in San Diego.

I immediately got really nervous because I didn't know any of the big league trainers. I didn't even know too many of the big league players at the time, as I was only twenty years old. I drove as fast as I could to the stadium, pulled in, and was completely unaware of what I was wearing.

I walked into the San Diego big league clubhouse with my New York Mets hat on. Tony Gwynn, Phil Nevin, and Ryan Klesko were there, sitting around and playing cards.

I went into the training room, and I kind of saw them talking about me as I walked in. Nervous, I sat down on the trainers' table and I told them who I was. They said to me, "Do you understand what you are doing?" I said, "What do you mean, I have permission to be in here." I thought that they were mad because I was in their clubhouse.

One of the trainers who I had already become friends with, because he was my rookie ball trainer, told me that I just walked in with a Mets hat on. Obviously, that was a no-no. So, as I was laying on the training table, Phil Nevin thought it would be funny to play a joke on me.

He came in, grabbed my Mets hat and said, "Why would you ever wear that hat in our clubhouse?" He was serious and I was scared as hell. I was almost in tears. As Phil disappeared, the trainers told me that I would never be forgiven, and my hat would probably be trashed or burnt. Little did I know, it was all just a prank. Nevin returned to the training room saying, "Don't you ever come in this clubhouse again with somebody else's stuff on and if you don't learn your lesson, I never want to see you again."

Now I was really scared, thinking how I didn't belong there and that I was really uncomfortable. The next thing I knew, in came a brand new big league San Diego Padres cap in my size. Phil came over and told me that the guys were just joking with me and that they knew who I was. He said that he knew I was young and that if he ever saw me again, that I better be wearing it.

Little did they know, I got on the roster the next year and I went into the clubhouse wearing the hat. They all busted out laughing, remembering the story and who I was.

I will certainly never forget that. As for the Mets hat, lets just say I have been wearing the Padres cap ever since.

Al Martin

Major League Clubs/Minor League Organizations:
TAMPA BAY DEVIL RAYS, SEATTLE MARINERS,
PITTSBURGH PIRATES, ATLANTA BRAVES

Position: OUTFIELD

Team: WEST PALM BEACH, FL

League: GULF COAST

Year: 1985

AL MARTIN played eleven seasons in the Major Leagues with Pittsburgh, San Diego, Seattle, and Tampa Bay, compiling a career batting average of .276 with 132 home runs and 485 RBI. In 1996, he set career highs by batting .300 with 40 doubles, 72 RBI, and 38 stolen bases while playing for the Pirates.

Martin played eight seasons in the Minor Leagues from 1985 to 1992. His memorable Minor League experience occurred while playing Class A ball in the Atlanta Braves organization.

The most memorable thing about the Minor Leagues to me was being in the Braves system, which was very competitive.

When we were in the instructional league, we would play every day. The guy who had the best day would get a chicken sandwich from Burger King. I know it may sound stupid, but back then we were probably making all of $10 a day in meal money. No one had any money, and the Burger King sandwiches were so good.

It was so important to guys that they would go out and have huge games over this sandwich. Guys like David Justice and Brian Hunter, guys who turned out to be good big leaguers. To this day when we see each other, we still laugh about those stories.

I think mentally, the Braves sense of competition was very important to us. It was only a chicken sandwich, but it could have been a big league contract.

Quinton McCracken

Major League Clubs/Minor League Organizations:
COLORADO ROCKIES, TAMPA BAY DEVIL RAYS,
MINNESOTA TWINS, ARIZONA DIAMONDBACKS,
SEATTLE MARINERS

Position: OUTFIELD

Team: BEND, OR

League: NORTHWEST

Year: 1992

QUINTON McCRACKEN has been a valuable outfielder for a few Major League teams throughout his career with his ability to switch-hit and play all three positions. His best overall season came as a member of the Tampa Bay Devil Rays during their inaugural season, batting .292 with seven home runs and 59 RBI in 155 games played. In 2002, McCracken helped lead the Arizona Diamondbacks to the postseason by hitting a career best .309.

McCracken played parts of five seasons in the Minor Leagues from 1992 to 2000. His memorable Minor League experience occurred while playing Class A ball in the Colorado Rockies organization.

It was 1992 and I was up in the Northwest League with the Bend Rockies.

That was the Rockies first professional baseball team. We were their first amateur draft and they were going to have the draft for the big league club that fall. We were pretty much the future Rockies, and so all of the eyes in Denver were on the kids that they just drafted.

We were traveling from Yakima, Washington, to Boise, Idaho, on a six-hour bus ride when the air conditioning went out. It was the hottest and most uncomfortable ride I ever experienced in professional baseball.

Guys stripped down to their underwear on the bus, sweating bullets, and we still had three or four hours to go. I remember thinking that if this was professional baseball, I may want to reconsider.

It was definitely one of those things where you wanted to continue to work hard so you did not repeat A ball.

Randy Choate

Major League Clubs/Minor League Organizations: NEW YORK YANKEES, MONTREAL EXPOS, ARIZONA DIAMONDBACKS

Position: PITCHER

Team: COLUMBUS, OH

League: INTERNATIONAL

Year: 2003

RANDY CHOATE played four seasons with the New York Yankees, compiling a 3–2 record with a 4.50 ERA in 82 games and 90 innings pitched. He established himself as the Yankees left-handed bullpen specialist during the 2001 World Series against the Arizona Diamondbacks, appearing in two games and throwing 3.2 innings with two strikeouts in one of the greatest Series ever.

Choate played parts of seven seasons in the Minor Leagues from 1997 to 2003. His memorable Minor League experience occurred while playing Class AAA ball in the New York Yankees organization.

I was with the Columbus Clippers and we were in Toledo, Ohio, which was the Tigers Minor League team.

About two weeks earlier, I had really changed my hairstyle. I used to have long hair, but I shaved my head down and dyed it blond. It basically looked like Eminem and was white!

I hardly ever wore my hat, just so I could get some sun on my head. I kind of liked my new hairdo, too.

It was a day game and I hadn't pitched in three or four days. I was standing around and we were blowing this team out, so I wasn't going to pitch that day. One of the other relievers, our closer, played a joke on me.

When I wasn't looking, being distracted by some of the guys, he put eye black on the inside of my hat. He put quite a bit in there, by where my ear was and on the top. We had dark blue hats, and you really couldn't see it unless you were looking for it. Well, I wasn't going to pitch, and this became a problem for them because they thought that I would get in the game.

So, they had to go up to the bullpen coach and get him to have me throw a bullpen. In about the seventh inning, the coach came up to me and told me that I wasn't going to get in the game but that I needed to throw because I hadn't thrown in three or four days. I said, "Okay, but I don't do this normally."

I threw my hat on, went out, and threw the bullpen. I was walking in toward the dugout with people smiling at me and I had no idea why. I was laughing, too. In the dugout, nobody told me about it and they were just trying not to laugh.

Drew Henson pulled me up to the top step of the dugout, looking out at the field where everyone in the stands could see me, and started talking to me. He was just trying to keep me out there. It wasn't until I got in the clubhouse after the game that I noticed that it was all over my head. I took my hat off and it left black marks everywhere. I looked like a leper.

At first, I thought about getting even. But by the time I got off the bus ride home, I got over it. The guys didn't want to tell me who did it because they thought I was going to retaliate. In the end, I didn't mind being laughed at.

Gil Patterson

Major League Clubs/Minor League Organizations:
NEW YORK YANKEES, TORONTO BLUE JAYS

Position: PITCHER/PITCHING COACH

Team: SYRACUSE, NY

League: INTERNATIONAL

Year: 1976

GIL PATTERSON was a rising star with the New York Yankees before arm injuries derailed his playing career. He reached the big leagues with the Yankees at twenty-one years old in 1977, appearing in 10 games and going 1–2 with a 5.45 ERA with the eventual World Champions. Gil became the pitching coach of the Toronto Blue Jays prior to the 2002 season, tutoring a staff that included Cy Young Award winners Roy Halladay and Pat Hentgen.

Patterson pitched seven seasons in the Minor Leagues from 1975 to 1983, missing two seasons altogether in 1978 and '79 due to a torn rotator cuff. His memorable Minor League experience occurred while playing Class AAA ball in the New York Yankees organization.

I was pretty lucky and God blessed me with a very good arm.

In my short time in the Minor Leagues, Bobby Cox helped me quite a bit in Triple-A. When he was my manager in Triple-A, he told me to trust my stuff, be aggressive, and go right after hitters.

That same season, I pitched in the Mayor's Trophy Game against the New York Mets. The game was in the summer and played at Yankee Stadium. I was only twenty years old. The Yankees brought Ron Guidry, Jim Beattie, and me for the game.

I pitched the same way that I did in the Minor Leagues, and it was six up and six down. Guidry gave up runs, Beattie gave up runs, and I shut them out. That was when I said to myself, "I'm ready."

Because of that, and when I went to my first big league camp in March of 1976 and struck out eight Orioles in three innings, the combination of those two things were the biggest factors in my trusting that I belonged in the Major Leagues.

Ray Durham

Major League Clubs/Minor League Organizations: SAN FRANCISCO GIANTS, CHICAGO WHITE SOX, OAKLAND ATHLETICS

Position: INFIELDER/OUTFIELDER

Team: UTICA, NY, OR SARASOTA, FL

League: NEW YORK-PENN OR FLORIDA STATE

Year: 1991 OR 1992

RAY DURHAM has been a significant asset to every team he has played for. A speedy and versatile infielder and outfielder, he has a lifetime batting average of .280 and has stolen at least 20 bases seven times in his career. In the 2002 Divisional Series with Oakland, he batted .333 with two home runs and two RBI over five games.

Durham spent five seasons in the Minor Leagues from 1990 to 1994. His memorable Minor League experience occurred while playing Class A ball in the Chicago White Sox organization.

It was 1991 or '92, and I was in the White Sox organization. I was with a bunch of guys that played a lot of pranks on the phone. An agent at the time called and I thought it was the guys screwing around. I hung up on the guy three or so times, and he kept calling back.

I finally said, "I wish you guys would stop playing jokes."

The agent said that this was not a joke, and that he was so and so. I said, "Yeah right, come on guys. Quit fooling around because I am getting tired of this." But he said, "No, I really am this guy and I want to go out to dinner and talk."

Sure enough, he ended up being my agent and he's still my agent to this day.

I really thought it was the guys messing around on the phone because I know that I would do it to them.

Shane Spencer

Major League Clubs/Minor League
Organizations: NEW YORK YANKEES,
CLEVELAND INDIANS, NEW YORK
METS

Position: OUTFIELDER

Team: TAMPA, FL

League: FLORIDA STATE

Year: 1995

SHANE SPENCER became one of the most popular home run hitters in the Major Leagues during the magical season of the home run chase in 1998. While he wasn't in contention with Mark McGuire and Sammy Sosa for the single-season home run record, he did belt 10 homers in 67 at-bats over 27 games after being called up to the New York Yankees from Triple-A Columbus. Spencer's success continued through the postseason, as he was a member of the Yankees historic World Championship club that won 125 games.

Spencer played parts of twelve seasons in the Minor Leagues from 1990 to 2001. His memorable Minor League experience occurred while playing Class A ball in the New York Yankees organization.

There were a bunch of influential people on me in the minors. My manager in the Florida State League, Jay Gibbs, was kind of old school. He really looked after me and just loved the way I played. He would say, "Boys, show up on time, play hard, and that's all I ask. The rest will take care of itself. Even if you're struggling, just play hard." I really remembered that.

There were so many outfielders in front of me that were prospects, the Yankees held me back in the Florida State League again after I had a pretty good year. It ended up working out pretty good because I wound up playing every single day, had a real good year, and fine-tuned myself in the outfield. Then I had another real good year the next year in Double-A.

I never had anything handed to me. When I made it, it made it that much more worthwhile because I earned it. I can honestly say that I earned making it to the big leagues.

I don't regret anything from the Minor Leagues, but the one thing that is missing at the big league level is the camaraderie that you had in the minors. You were with each other all the time, sharing rooms or being on the bus, and you would become lifelong friends with those guys.

I miss that.

Jason Michaels

Major League Clubs/Minor League
Organizations: PHILADELPHIA PHILLIES

Position: OUTFIELDER

Team: BATAVIA, NY

League: NEW YORK-PENN

Year: 1998

JASON MICHAELS broke into the
Major Leagues in 2001 and has been a
very valuable player for the Phillies since that point. As a fourth outfielder
with the club in 2003, he batted .330 with five home runs and 17 RBI in
81 games. As a result of his success, his playing time increased in 2004 and
he set career highs with 115 games played, 10 home runs, and 40 RBI.

Michaels played parts of five seasons in the Minor Leagues from 1998
to 2002. His memorable Minor League experience occurred while playing Class A ball in the Philadelphia Phillies organization.

My parents came up at the end of July, and they were there
for a week during a home stand.

I was struggling, hitting .084 after 120 at-bats. I think I had
all of 12 hits. I was the highest draft pick on the team and I was
embarrassing. I couldn't hit. It was a joke. But, I never blew up
about it. Everybody thought I was psycho for not doing that.

So, on August 2, the day before my parents were supposed
to leave, we were playing the Pirates team from Erie. I ended
up hitting my first home run of the season, which was a grand
slam.

Well, I went on that month to hit 11 more home runs in
August and hit about .450. I was the Player of the Month for
the organization and ended up bringing my average up to
almost .270.

That home run was a real starting point, to help me figure
it out a little bit in pro ball.

Dave Wallace

Major League Clubs/Minor League Organizations:
PHILADELPHIA PHILLIES, TORONTO BLUE JAYS,
LOS ANGELES DODGERS, NEW YORK METS,
BOSTON RED SOX

Position: PITCHER

Team: SPARTANBURG, SC

League: SOUTH ATLANTIC

Year: 1970

DAVE WALLACE is regarded as one of the best pitching coaches in base-ball. As the pitching coach of the Boston Red Sox in 2004, he helped lead Boston to its first World Series title since 1918 by tutoring a staff that included Curt Schilling, Pedro Martinez, Derek Lowe, Tim Wakefield, and Keith Foulke. Wallace also served as the pitching coach of the Los Angeles Dodgers and the New York Mets, leading both clubs to the postseason during his tenure and guiding the Mets to the World Series in 2000.

Wallace played parts of ten seasons in the Minor Leagues from 1970 to 1979. His memorable Minor League experience occurred while play-ing Class A ball in the Philadelphia Phillies organization.

In 1970 at spring training with the Phillies, I think that I was number 136 or something.

I think what hit me first was the number of people. I said, "Oh my god! What kind of odds do I have here?" I was a guy that was not a high draft pick, a guy on the smaller side, and a guy that didn't throw 96 mph. I knew I was up against some tough odds.

The first town I ever played in was Spartanburg, South Carolina. On opening night, I got the starting assignment. I think we won the game like 7–6 or 8–7 and I believe that I got the win. It wasn't anything earth-shattering.

But what I remember more than anything was after the game, looking into the mirror and saying, "Hey, you know what, this is just baseball. It's just like we play anywhere. It's not any different."

I think that Jim Bunning was the most influential person on me in the Minor Leagues. I played for Jim when he quit playing and became a manager. I played for him for four years in Eugene, Oregon, in the Pacific Coast League and Toledo, Ohio, in the International League.

Jim was a sharp, honest guy that called them as he saw them. He taught me a lot about pitching, a lot about baseball, a lot about life, and a lot about desire and attitude.

I got finished playing at the end of 1979 and had a chance to coach for the Phillies right away. But I decided to just stay at home with my family and try working for a living. I had a college degree and started working in a shop. We made some kind of alloys and metals.

Then, I put some résumés out and got a call from the Dodgers. I went out for an interview and they offered me the job on the spot. I said to myself that it was the Dodgers and that I didn't know anybody, so if I was going to get into coaching, I just assume start somewhere and make it on my own reputation.

I later coached at every level because I was the Dodgers Minor League pitching coordinator. I first came across Pedro Martinez in the late 1980s and had a good relationship with Ramon Martinez at that point. They both signed with us out of our baseball academy in the Dominican Republic. So, I was involved with both of them at every level, every step of the way.

Pedro was a stubborn little guy who really believed in himself. He was just Ramon's little brother. He kind of took offense to that and wanted to prove everybody wrong. He was a lot smaller but had just as good stuff. You want that good kind of cockiness and arrogance that goes into being a pitcher.

There are a lot of things that I am proud of from my time developing players in the Minor Leagues. There was Hersheiser, the Martinezes, and John Wetteland.

We made Wetteland into a short reliever at the Triple-A level, and unfortunately we traded him, but he went on to become a pretty damn good closer in the big leagues. There was John Franco, who Guy Conti and I got involved with in developing his change up.

But Brian Holden, who is probably a name that nobody really knows about, was a five- or six-year Triple-A guy when I was the Triple-A pitching coach in Albuquerque.

We got into it pretty good one night and I finally said to him, "Hey, I know that you are having success here and you're doing good in Triple-A. But unless you change things, you are going to stay here."

Well, he went on to pitch three or four years in the big leagues and was on the 1988 championship team with the Dodgers.

Walt Hriniak

Major League Clubs/Minor League Organizations:
MILWAUKEE BRAVES,
ATLANTA BRAVES,
SAN DIEGO PADRES

Position: CATCHER/HITTING COACH

Team: WEST PALM BEACH, FL

League: SPRING TRAINING

Year: 1968

WALT HRINIAK is considered to be one of the most influential hitting coaches in Major League baseball. Having spent time in that role with the Boston Red Sox and Chicago White Sox, Hriniak was responsible for developing hitting stars such as Wade Boggs, Frank Thomas, and Robin Ventura.

Hriniak played eleven seasons in the Minor Leagues from 1961 to 1971. His memorable Minor League experience occurred while playing Class AA ball in the Milwaukee Braves organization.

One particular story was in 1968 in spring training.
I had played since '61 and gone from a prospect to a suspect. They turned me into a catcher in 1968 and that was when I first came in contact with Charlie Lau.

He had just got done playing with the Braves and was going to manage Shreveport, Louisiana, of the Texas League. The first day of spring training, we went to the batting cage down the left-field foul line in West Palm Beach.

We were all taking swings off of the pitching machine, and it was the first time Charlie Lau had ever seen me swing a bat. So I got in the batting cage, and I hit every ball right on the button. But I pulled every one of them to the right side of the field because I was a left-hand hitter. Every ball that I hit, I felt like I was showing this guy something.

Anyway, after fifteen, twenty, thirty swings he said, "That's it, last swing." I took one more and hit it right on the button again and got out of the cage. I thought I had done a pretty good job and said to him, "Well, what did you think of that, Charlie?"

He looked at me dead in the eyes and said, "Well, one thing about it, Walter, they'll know where to play you."

That was my introduction to Charlie. Charlie was the kind of guy who believed in moving the ball around and hitting it to the opposite field, not just pulling the ball.

That was certainly one story in my Minor League career that I will never forget.

Matt Mantei

Major League Clubs/Minor League Organizations:
SEATTLE MARINERS, FLORIDA MARLINS,
ARIZONA DIAMONDBACKS

Position: PITCHER

Team: BELLINGHAM, WA

League: NORTHWEST

Year: 1993

MATT MANTEI established himself as the closer of the Arizona Diamondbacks in 1999, recording 22 saves and helping them advance to the postseason for the first time in franchise history. In five seasons with the Diamondbacks from 1999 to 2003, he saved 70 games and was a member of the 2001 World Series Champions.

Mantei played parts of eleven seasons in the Minor Leagues from 1991 to 2002. His memorable Minor League experience occurred while playing Class A ball in the Seattle Mariners organization.

We were in Bellingham, Washington, in 1993. We won our division and went on to the playoffs.

Boise, Idaho, which was like an eighteen-hour bus trip from where we were, came to town. They played us that night and beat us in the first game of a best-out-of-three.

We got on a bus and drove eighteen hours to play the next day in Idaho. We got whooped like 13–2 and had to get back on the bus to drive eighteen hours back. So, we spent thirty-six hours on the bus to go out and get our asses whooped by Boise.

It was a big letdown. To go all the way out there just to get worked, it was very frustrating.

Craig Dingman

Major League Clubs/Minor League Organizations: NEW YORK YANKEES, COLORADO ROCKIES, CINCINNATI REDS, CHICAGO CUBS, DETROIT TIGERS

Position: PITCHER

Team: NORWICH, CT

League: EASTERN

Year: 1999

CRAIG DINGMAN is a great example of hard work and determination paying off. After spending most of his professional career in the minors, he pitched in 24 games for the Detroit Tigers in 2004 and was 2–2 out of the bullpen. Since 1994, Dingman has thrown 463 Minor League innings and compiled 551 strikeouts.

Dingman played parts of ten seasons in the Minor Leagues from 1994 to 2004. His memorable Minor League experience occurred while playing Class AA ball in the New York Yankees organization.

W hen I was in Norwich, there was a thick wooded area behind the outfield wall of the stadium.

Some of the guys would go back there with their .22s and shoot rabbits and frogs before and after the game. We would just mess around. One day, Nick Johnson asked us about road hunting and going with us. So, we asked him to come with us and hang out.

He was all into it and pumped up, thinking he was going to do something. When we got him back into the trees and stuff, he asked me, "What happens if a farmer or someone comes after us and says something?"

I said, "Dude, if a farmer comes out, they usually shoot first and ask questions later. So, if they come out shooting, just start running and get out of here."

A buddy of mine from the team and I set it up where we were going to walk down this trail and up to a creek bed where there was a big wall of concrete. He would sit at the top with my .357 pistol and imitate a farmer.

We were all walking through the trees. Nick was on the spotlight, having a good time. Just as we got up to the creek bed by the concrete, I took it from him and started spotlighting. It was pitch black.

Suddenly, my teammate stood up with a Maglite from about twenty yards away. I turned my spotlight off and said, "Nick, it's a farmer." My teammate yelled, "Get off my land you sons of bitches!" and starting shooting my .357 in the air. I ducked down and said, "Nick, duck! They're shooting at us! They're shooting at us!"

Before I could turn around, he was trying to run through the trees. He was running into evergreens and falling back down. The next thing I knew, he was just running down the trail. He looked like Pee Wee from Porky's. The dude was just flying, knocking trees out of the way and everything.

He went back to the clubhouse, got in the shower with his shorts and his T-shirt on and took a cold shower. He had little scrapes from the bushes all over him. He was pretty much shaking, and I think we scared the hell out of him.

We didn't tell him until the next day, but one of our other teammates there with us told him that night. He said that he had to tell him because Nick was all shook up. He said that Nick kept looking out the window for a farmer who might have followed him home.

David Walling

Major League Clubs/Minor League Organizations:
NEW YORK YANKEES

Position: PITCHER

Team: STATEN ISLAND, NY

League: NEW YORK-PENN

Year: 1999

DAVID WALLING was a first-round draft choice of the New York Yankees in 1999. He compiled a 24–24 record in 58 games started at four
Minor League levels, reaching Triple-A Columbus in just two and a half
seasons. His pinpoint control and ability to strike out batters made him a
top prospect in the organization, but he surprised the Yankees and baseball insiders when he elected to abruptly retire from baseball at age
twenty-four.

Walling played four seasons in the Minor Leagues from 1999 to 2002.
His memorable Minor League experience occurred while playing Class A
ball in the New York Yankees organization.

W hen I first signed in 1999, I came out of the University
of Arkansas.

I was drafted in the first round by the New York Yankees, so
it was kind of a big deal. I went to Florida to their camp site,
and then they shipped us off to Staten Island. It was the first time
the team played in Staten Island.

We showed up in New York at about 2 A.M. I was from San
Diego and had never really been east of Arkansas. When we got
to our apartment complex, which were just pigsties, they gave
us a key and told us to go find our apartment. So, there was an
entire team of guys walking around at 2:30 A.M. trying to figure
out what apartment they belonged to.

I finally found my apartment with my two roommates. Now,
that part is important, because notice that I said my two
roommates.

We walked into our apartment, which was a basement apartment by the way, and the first thing that we saw was an overturned, wood pallet couch with no cushions on it. It just had a wood frame.

I walked into the first bedroom and saw that there was a single bed. I was 6'5", 225 pounds. After I noticed the single bed, I thought to myself, "Damn, who is going to get that bed?"

I suddenly realized that was the only bedroom in the whole apartment. So, we had three big guys, a one-bedroom apartment, one single bed, and one wood frame couch without cushions turned over. When I went to go to use the restroom, I found that there was no toilet seat.

So, I had to just squat down to go to the bathroom. My roommate walked in laughing because we had such terrible accommodations. We were thinking that because we played for the Yankees now, we were going to be "big-time." As we were talking and laughing, a cockroach fell on his shoulder to top off the evening.

That night, we put the single bed in the middle of the living room with our luggage around it to form a barrier. All three of us slept fully clothed on the single bed.

The next day, almost everyone was bitching. Some people had a three-bedroom, so they were okay with it. Other people had a two-bedroom. Then there was us.

We were just barking up a storm. They ended up finding a two-bedroom apartment for us, which wasn't that bad. I would have liked to have had my own room but I wasn't that spoiled.

The apartment did not have air conditioning, and that summer in New York was hot! There was a stretch for like fifteen straight days where it was 100 degrees.

At this point, we were just dying to go on a road trip because we wanted to stay in a hotel so bad. We went to Utica, New York.

When we got to Utica, they were renovating the hotel that we were staying in, which was par for the course in the Minor

Leagues. As they were renovating the hotel, there were mattresses all over the corridors of this place.

My mind went right to work. I went to the front desk and
asked the manager for one of the mattresses that they were
throwing away. He said that was fine, and so I stuffed a queen
mattress underneath our bus. It was bowed under the bus
because it wouldn't fit right. It took up so much space, I had to
carry people's bags and put them in my seat.

I took it back to Staten Island so that I could have a queen
bed. I was the only player with a queen bed the entire summer.

Three days later, it was our home opener. I pitched the
home opener and New York Mayor Rudy Giuliani came out to
the mound to throw out the first pitch with me.

That was the funny thing about the Minor Leagues, the ups
and downs.

One day, I was living in this crappy apartment, sleeping on
a bed that I took from a hotel in Utica and brought back on the
bus. The next day, I was throwing out the first pitch with the
mayor of New York.

Wade Boggs

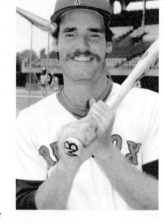

Major League Clubs/Minor League
Organizations: BOSTON RED SOX,
NEW YORK YANKEES, TAMPA BAY
DEVIL RAYS

Position: THIRD BASE

Team: PAWTUCKET, RI

League: INTERNATIONAL

Year: 1981

WADE BOGGS is one of the greatest hitters in baseball history. The future Hall of Famer hit at least .300 in fourteen of fifteen straight seasons, including ten consecutive years from 1982 to 1991. The twelve-time All-Star finished his career with a .328 average and 3,010 hits. He won the American League batting title five times, led the league in on-base percentage six times, and captured two Gold Glove Awards. He won a World Series championship with the New York Yankees in 1996 and played in nine postseason series.

Boggs played six seasons in the Minor Leagues from 1976 to 1981. His memorable Minor League experience occurred while playing Class AAA ball in the Boston Red Sox organization.

Author's Note: On April, 18, 1981, the Rochester Red Wings of the Baltimore Orioles organization and the Pawtucket Red Sox of the Boston Red Sox organization played the longest game in professional baseball history. The game lasted more than eight hours and was stopped at 4:07 A.M. with the scored tied 2–2 after thirty-two innings. It was completed on June 23, 1981, and won by the Red Sox 3–2 in the bottom of the thirty-third inning at Pawtucket's McCoy Stadium.

The most memorable part of the thirty-three inning game was the length of it. There was no curfew or time limit. It was played on Easter Eve weekend, was 28 or 30 degrees out, and the wind was blowing in from left.

I hit a double to tie up the game up in the twenty-first inning. After that, no one was going to score again because it was so cold. I remember every at-bat in that game. I was 4-for-12.

It was one crazy thing after another. Once we got to about 2:30 or 3:00 A.M., it sort of got to the ridiculous stage but we just kept playing.

There were a lot of little things that went on during that game. Joe Morgan, our manager, got ejected in the third or fourth inning. He had to hang around behind the fence by the dugout to "manage" from back there. He stayed behind the fence for almost all thirty-three innings.

At around 3:30, we started building bonfires in the dugout with broken bats. We were begging guys to break bats just so that we could have a little bit of warmth.

There were approximately eleven or thirteen fans left at the end of the game. My wife and daughter were still there and my daughter was sleeping under PawSox owner Ben Mondor's desk in his office. I believe that he gave season tickets to the people that were left.

When the game was called, the guys were relieved that there wasn't a loser after going that far. Guys were also relieved just to go home and get a little shut-eye because we had to be back at the ballpark at 11 A.M. We had a day game the next day, and consequently, I believe that the game the next day went seventeen innings. In two days, we played about a week's worth of games.

We thought that when we came back to the ballpark the next day, we would continue the thirty-two innings we had played. It was decided that they would save it until the next time Rochester came in.

Because Major League Baseball was on strike when they came back in, we had people there from Japan, the United Kingdom, Europe, and the United States just to cover the game. Ironically, it only went one inning.

When baseball went on strike, Major League Baseball wanted us to go up to Fenway Park and finish the game there. We decided as Minor League players that we were not going to do that and cross the picket lines. We would just finish the game at McCoy.

Dave Roberts

Major League Clubs/Minor League Organizations:
DETROIT TIGERS, CLEVELAND INDIANS,
LOS ANGELES DODGERS, BOSTON RED SOX

Position: CENTER FIELD

Team: JAMESTOWN, NY

League: NEW YORK-PENN

Year: 1994

DAVE ROBERTS stole the most important base in Boston Red Sox history. Down three games to none and trailing 4–3 in the bottom of the ninth inning in Game 4 of the 2004 American League Championship Series against the New York Yankees, Roberts pinch ran at first base, stole second, and scored the tying run on a base hit to spark the greatest comeback ever in Major League baseball. Subsequently, he helped lead the Red Sox to a World Series Championship. Over the past three seasons, he has swiped 123 bases with the Red Sox and Los Angeles Dodgers.

Roberts played parts of eight seasons in the Minor Leagues from 1994 to 2001. His memorable Minor League experience occurred while playing Class A ball in the Detroit Tigers organization.

I remember the lifestyle that a Minor Leaguer led. For me, I was in Jamestown, New York, in the New York-Penn League during my rookie ball year.

My roommates and I, when we would be on the road in different clubhouses, would grab a bunch of toilet paper and stuff it in our bags. We couldn't afford to buy toilet paper because we were making like $900 per month.

We would take things that you would need around the house but couldn't afford, like soap. I was in charge of the toilet paper, another roommate was in charge of getting soap, another roommate was in charge of detergent and stuff like that.

Now, with guys making a lot of money, it makes you appreciate what you have. But, my first paycheck was $353 after taxes.

The next year, I went to the Florida State League and got bumped up in pay $150 per month. That was huge money then. You would get paid five months out of the year, and so now I was making about $5,000.

I thought I was the big cheese back then.

Mike Barnett

Major League Clubs/Minor League Organizations: CHICAGO WHITE SOX, TORONTO BLUE JAYS

Position: HITTING COACH

Team: BIRMINGHAM, AL

League: SOUTHERN

Year: 1993–1994

MIKE BARNETT was named the hitting coach of the Toronto Blue Jays prior to the 2002 season. In 2003, the Blue Jays finished second in the American League in batting average, slugging percentage, hits, and runs batted in. He has tutored sluggers Carlos Delgado, Eric Hinske, and Vernon Wells on a daily basis.

Barnett worked and coached for twenty seasons in the Minor Leagues from 1982 to 2001. His memorable Minor League experience occurred while coaching Class AA ball in the Chicago White Sox organization.

I think that the two most memorable experiences that I had in the Minor Leagues were in 1993 and 1994 with the White Sox in Birmingham, Alabama.

The first experience was coaching Michael Jordan in 1994. I think any time you are a coach and get to work with someone who was an absolute elite athlete as he was, you are never going to forget that.

The biggest thing that I will remember about Michael is I still have never seen anybody with a work ethic like he had. A determined, willing desire to get better every day. Here's a guy who, yes, had tremendous athletic ability but with very limited baseball experience. He played in high school, hadn't played for fourteen years and was a pitcher. Now hearing everyone looking back saying that Michael Jordan was a flop as a baseball player, I say just the opposite.

I think he was a tremendous success. To look at what he had to go through after being at such a high pinnacle of his athletic career in the NBA, and to take on that challenge and to see how he tackled that challenge and handled it, it was something that I will never forget. I tell people that the strides that he made and to step into Double-A baseball with virtually no experience and do what he did was amazing.

After the season was over, he went to the Arizona Fall League. I will never forget sitting at home in Knoxville and getting a phone call from Michael. He asked me what I was doing, and I told him that I was just sitting around and relaxing. I asked him how it was going, and he told me that he needed me to come out there. I said when do you want me to come out, next week or what? He said, "No. Tomorrow!"

He then asked me if I could get on the horn and see what flights I could get. I told him sure. I called him back and told him that the flights were ridiculous, from $1,100 to $1,200. He said, "I don't care what they cost, just get out here tomorrow!" I went out there, and we just resumed some of our work against better competition.

He ended up hitting about .255 in the fall league. I look back on the whole thing and say if he went to college as a baseball player, he would have been another Dave Winfield.

Initially, I think some of our players thought here was this guy coming in and getting all this attention and he's not really even a baseball player. But I think the players then saw the way he approached and went about his business day in and day out and attempted to deflect the attention away from himself. Then, the thing that I think the players loved was we played in front of tremendous crowds in Birmingham and went on the road sold out every night.

To go through that experience without a great club that finished at about .500, it was kind of a traveling show. What gets lost in that entire situation was Michael Jordan the person. How he touched so many people's lives. I always marveled at how he treated people, his work ethic, his determination, his drive. It's no wonder that he has been as successful as he's been throughout his career.

I also remember the tremendous set-up and situation we had in 1993. To have won the Southern League Championship and to be a part of that club was something special. It was one of those rare situations in the Minor Leagues where we kept the club together almost the whole year.

The other two coaches that were there, Terry Francona, who is now managing the Boston Red Sox, and Curt Champion, who is now the pitching coordinator for the White Sox, have remained unbelievable friends of mine.

We didn't have a lot of big-name players, although we had some pretty good pitching, I think our biggest name position player was Ray Durham. To beat who we beat, which was the Knoxville Blue Jays, and be on the other side of the field of Carlos Delgado, Shawn Green, and other tremendous players, was an incredible accomplishment.

To look back and see the friends and relationships that you develop kind of encompasses the whole Minor League experience. Coming together, winning a championship and keeping a club together the whole year was phenomenal.

Edgardo Alfonzo

Major League Clubs/Minor League
Organizations: NEW YORK METS,
SAN FRANCISCO GIANTS

Position: THIRD BASE

Team: BINGHAMTON, NY

League: EASTERN

Year: 1994

EDGARDO ALFONZO broke into the
Major Leagues as a twenty-one-year-old
hard-hitting infielder with the New York Mets. He quickly became one of
the best overall third basemen in 1999 and 2000, when the All-Star hit over
.300 with 52 home runs and 202 RBI in those two playoff years for the
Mets. In ten big league seasons, he has a career average of .288 with 144
homers and 696 RBI.

Alfonzo played four seasons in the Minor Leagues from 1991 to 1994.
His memorable Minor League experience occurred while playing Class AA
ball in the New York Mets organization.

I was in Double-A with Binghamton, and we were coming back
from a road trip from I don't know where.

Then, the bus driver got stung by a bee near his eye. That made
his eye swell up and the bus driver couldn't see out of his eye!

Everyone was trying to figure out how it happened. Why was
this guy's eye like that and why couldn't he drive?

It was about an eight-hour trip back home, and we had to
wait for about an hour for another bus driver to come and take
us back to Binghamton.

Butch Hobson

Major League Clubs/Minor League Organizations:
BOSTON RED SOX, CALIFORNIA ANGELS,
NEW YORK YANKEES

Position: THIRD BASE, MANAGER

Team: CAPITAL CITY, SC

League: SOUTH ATLANTIC

Year: 1987

BUTCH HOBSON played eight seasons in the Major Leagues with three teams. The best season of his career was in 1977, when he hit 30 home runs and drove in 112 RBI with the Boston Red Sox. A quarterback in college at the University of Alabama, Butch paved the way for the prominent two-sport athlete. He also managed three seasons for Boston and compiled 207 wins.

Hobson played two seasons in the Minor Leagues from 1973 to 1974 and has managed since 1985. His memorable Minor League experience occurred while managing Class A ball in the New York Mets organization.

I was never tossed out of a game as a player, ever. All the years that I played, I never argued with umpires. If the umpire blew the call, I just accepted it and went on. That's just the way that I was.

When I first started managing, I thought that was what you were supposed to do. The manager had to stick up for his players. After I got myself kicked out of a game for the first time and saw the fans get excited about it, I thought that this was not so bad after all.

I was managing in the Mets system in Columbia, South Carolina, in 1987, and we were playing in the bottom of the twelfth inning. Our dugout was down the right-field line in Columbia, and there was a call at first base on the back end of a double play.

We had runners at first and third with one out in a tied game. The runner on the back end of the double play was called out by the umpire even though he was clearly safe. The run from third didn't score because it was a double play to end the inning.

I got into a heated argument and proceeded to get tossed out of the game after my tantrum. Bob Apodaca was my pitching coach, so I took the line-up over and gave it to him. As I was walking by, I said, "What the hell, I'll just take the base with me." So I went out and took first base to the locker room with me.

I went into my office and sat down at my desk. I was having a cigarette when General Manager Bill Blackwell came in and said, "Butch, we need the base." I said, "You're not getting it." He then said, "But we only have three bases."

Now, they really only had three bases. This was a small A ball operation. I told him again that he wasn't getting the base, and he told me that they couldn't start the game until he got it back. It was already about 11:30 P.M. I said that I would bring it back out there in a few minutes, which I wasn't supposed to do.

The Mets' colors were orange and blue, and they had just painted our locker room. The lockers were blue and had some orange trim on them. They were actually pretty ugly. Well, there just so happened to be a can of spray paint lying there, and it was that really bright orange. So I spray painted the base, the entire base bright orange.

I took it back out to the field, and the people that were left there gave me a standing ovation. The umpires didn't think too much of it. I went to out first base, put it back in the ground and said, "See if you can see this, you son of a bitch."

That cost me $450. At the end of the year, the booster club gave me that base, and I still have it to this day.

Sandy Alomar, Jr.

Major League Clubs/Minor League Organizations:
CLEVELAND INDIANS, CHICAGO WHITE SOX,
COLORADO ROCKIES, SAN DIEGO PADRES

Position: CATCHER

Team: BEAUMONT, TX

League: TEXAS

Year: 1986

SANDY ALOMAR, JR. redefined the position of catcher with his power-ful and imposing 6-5, 235-pound frame. In seventeen Major League sea-sons, the six-time All-Star has caught 1,237 games and posted a batting average of .273 with 111 home runs and 557 RBI. His best season came in 1997, when he batted .324 with 21 home runs and 83 RBI, and was voted the All-Star Game MVP after hitting a two-run homer in the American League's 3–1 victory at Jacobs Field in Cleveland. Later that season, his eighth-inning home run off of New York closer Mariano Rivera in Game 4 of the Divisional Series led the Indians past the Yankees and into the ALCS and World Series. In 1990, Alomar won the American League Rookie of the Year Award.

Alomar played parts of six seasons in the Minor Leagues from 1984 to 1989. His memorable Minor League experience occurred while play-ing Class A ball in the San Diego Padres organization.

When I played in Double-A in Beaumont, Texas, it was just terrible. The bus rides were long, it was hotter than crap and they had mosquitos there the size of jets. You had to go out to the field with a can of Off in your pocket to shag fly balls. It was pretty bad but that was what you knew. I had an idea about the big leagues, because my father played in the big leagues, but in the minors, you played your butt off because that was what you knew.

We had to share the locker room with a college team, Lamar University. When we went on the road, we had to take things out so that the college team could put things in. It was the worst ball-park I had ever played in.

There were far more things that you had to go through off the field than on the field. Yeah, guys are making millions of dollars these days, but people have no clue what those guys went through in the Minor Leagues.

On the field, that was the most fun part of the whole thing. You were getting paid to play, having fun and busy concentrating on playing the game. But off the field, you worried about what you were eating, sleeping on the floor, and stuff like that.

In Double-A, my brother Robbie and I lived together in Wichita, Kansas, after Beaumont moved to Wichita in 1987. We had a one-bedroom apartment with a couch and a bed. We set it up where whoever had had the best game got to sleep in the bed that night.

Do you know how many times I got to sleep in the bed? Not many. Robbie was leading the league in hitting for a long time. I did pretty well that year, but he slept in the bed a lot more than I did. I had to sleep on the couch a lot.

Roberto Alomar

Major League Clubs/Minor League Organizations:
SAN DIEGO PADRES, TORONTO BLUE JAYS, BALTIMORE ORIOLES, CLEVELAND INDIANS, NEW YORK METS, CHICAGO WHITE SOX, ARIZONA DIAMONDBACKS

Position: SECOND BASE

Team: WICHITA, KS

League: TEXAS

Year: 1987

ROBERTO ALOMAR is one of the best second basemen in baseball history and dominated the position throughout the 1990s. The twelve-time All-Star batted at least .300 nine times in a ten-year span from 1992 to 2001 and won two World Series rings with Toronto. In 1992, he was named the Most Valuable Player of the American League Championship Series en route to the Blue Jays first World Series title. The ten-time Gold Glove Award winner has a career batting average of .301 with over 200 home runs, 1,100 RBI, and 475 stolen bases.

Alomar played parts of four seasons in the Minor Leagues from 1985 to 1988. His memorable Minor League experience occurred while playing Class AA ball in the San Diego Padres organization.

With Sandy being the older brother, you had to respect whatever he said.

Whoever had the best game got to sleep in the bed. We had a one-bedroom apartment then. One time, Sandy's girlfriend came to town for two or three weeks. So, I had to sleep in the living room for about three weeks. I remember that I played pretty good during that time, but back then you really didn't mind. You just wanted to play.

My dad and my brother helped me a lot when I was coming up in the Minor Leagues. My dad was my first coach when I started playing in the Minor Leagues in Charlestown, South Carolina, in 1985.

My brother and I would push each other to get better and to develop as people. It was tough sometimes being Latin because we were there playing alone for so long. We had never been in that type of environment with Americans. I knew a little bit of English, but I didn't know a lot. I learned the basics of English in school.

But, that is why it was much easier for me when I had my dad and my brother there, because they really helped me a lot back then.

Andy Beal

Major League Clubs/Minor League
Organizations: NEW YORK YANKEES

Position: PITCHER

Team: TAMPA, FL

League: FLORIDA STATE

Year: 2001

ANDY BEAL is knocking on the door to
the Major Leagues. After quickly rising
through the New York Yankees organization in his first three seasons,
compiling a 27–17 record with a 3.15 ERA with Staten Island, Greensboro,
Tampa, Norwich, and Columbus, he has spent the past two years pitching at the Triple-A level. The twenty-five-year-old southpaw was a fifth-
round pick of the Yankees in the June 2000 draft out of Vanderbilt.

Beal has played parts of five seasons in the Minor Leagues from 2000
to 2004. His memorable Minor League experience occurred while playing Class A ball in the New York Yankees organization.

In 2001, I was in the Florida State League with the Tampa Yankees on a great team with a bunch of great guys.

We swept the first round of the playoffs, winning the first two
games of a best-of-three series. In the finals, we played against
Brevard County. The first game was played there, and we won.

So, we came back across the state to play in Tampa. We
ended up losing the next game and had one game left to decide
the championship.

Most of the guys were staying at Mr. Steinbrenner's hotel in
Tampa, the Radisson Bay Harbor. The morning of the final
game, September 11, I was getting out of the shower when my
cell phone rang.

It was Danny Borrell asking me if I had turned the televi-
sion on yet. Obviously, like everyone else, I saw what was going

on in the country. I sat there for the rest of the day and watched what went on.

To even think about a baseball game that night was just the last thing on anybody's mind. I don't think we even went to the park that day, and we actually sat around for a few more days without playing. Baseball was the last thing on the minds of everyone. Guys would go to the field to play catch, but we didn't do anything formal.

Our manager, Brian Butterfield, came in to tell us that the league decided to declare us co-champions so that we could go home to be with our families.

It was the only time in my career where I really didn't want to play. Baseball is such a great game and I want to play it every day, but not then. To know what so many people were going through, and what the country was going through, who cared about who won the 2001 Florida State League Championship.

It really put things into perspective.

Chone Figgins

Major League Clubs/Minor League Organizations:
COLORADO ROCKIES, ANAHEIM ANGELS

Position: SECOND BASE, THIRD BASE

Team: RALEIGH, NC

League: SOUTHERN

Year: 2001

CHONE FIGGINS is one of baseball's most exciting players to watch. In 2004, he batted .296 and finished third in the American League in stolen bases with 34 and second in triples with 17. In 698 career Minor League games, Figgins stole 208 bases and hit 66 triples.

Figgins played parts of seven seasons in the Minor Leagues from 1997 to 2003. His memorable Minor League experience occurred while playing Class AA ball in the Colorado Rockies organization.

In Double-A, I played in Raleigh, North Carolina, for the Carolina Mudcats. It was the worst place I ever played.

Our clubhouse was a trailer and we had maybe two showers. It was very small. It rained a lot there, and we did not have an indoor batting cage.

We had an outdoor cage, which was right under the bleachers, and so the rain would leak through into the cage. A lot of times, we wouldn't take batting practice or take ground balls. There was also nothing to eat after the games. Even if you tried to drive home and find something, there was still nowhere to eat.

But, we won the championship that year and I got a ring. That helped me, because coming up through the minors, it said that you were a winner.

That year really made me realize how much I loved the game. No matter how bad the conditions were, I still got my work in somehow, worked hard and tried to get better.

Carlos Delgado

Major League Clubs/Minor League
Organizations: TORONTO BLUE JAYS

Position: FIRST BASE

Team: ST. CATHARINES, ONTARIO,
CANADA

League: NEW YORK-PENN

Year: 1989

CARLOS DELGADO is one of the most dominating offensive players in Major League baseball. The two-time All-Star has hit more than 30 home runs every season since 1997 and has hit more than 40 long balls three times during that span. In 2003, Delgado finished second in the American League Most Valuable Player voting after batting .302 with 42 home runs and 145 RBI. He is also the Blue Jays all-time leader in home runs, grand slams, RBI, runs scored, and walks.

Delgado played parts of seven seasons in the Minor Leagues from 1989 to 1995. His memorable Minor League experience occurred while playing Class A ball in the Toronto Blue Jays organization.

I remember my first year of pro ball in 1989.

We played in Saint Catharines, Ontario, in the New York-Penn League. We all use to ride bikes, ten-speed bikes, that we rented for $25 per month. That was how we got to the ballpark.

In 1990, I ended up going back to the same league and went back to the same shop to get my bike. The guy who rented the bikes realized that it was a good gig for him, and was now renting the bikes for $50.

That was a lot of money then, because I was making about $800 per month and $11 a day in meal money on the road. I would have two or three roommates to try to split things as best we could.

I like to tell that story because people always say that big leaguers have it made, but in my first year, I had to ride a bike. Interesting.

Derek Jeter

Major League Clubs/Minor League
Organizations: NEW YORK YANKEES

Position: SHORTSTOP

Team: TAMPA, FL

League: GULF COAST LEAGUE

Year: 1992

DEREK JETER is simply one of the greatest players of all time. Over his ten-year Major League career, he has a .315 batting average with 150 home runs, 693 RBI, 1,037 runs scored, and 201 stolen bases. In 1999, he produced his best season yet with a .349 batting average, 24 home runs, and 102 RBI. The 1996 American League Rookie of the Year has led the New York Yankees to the World Series six times and the playoffs every year. The six-time All-Star has played in 99 postseason games, batting .314 with 13 home runs and 33 RBI. Jeter was also named the 2000 World Series MVP and All-Star Game MVP. In 2004, he earned his first Gold Glove Award.

Jeter played parts of four seasons in the Minor Leagues from 1992 to 1995. His memorable Minor League experience occurred while playing Class A ball in the New York Yankees organization.

For me, going from Kalamazoo to Florida, I went from playing baseball where the competition really wasn't that great to playing against the best players in the world from all different countries.

I was playing with second basemen and third basemen who didn't speak any English, and we didn't have any way to communicate. It was a real culture shock when I first started.

Being away from home, and struggling, was difficult for me. I had never been away from home before. In high school, I didn't really struggle that much. I went from hitting .500 or something to .200 and making errors all the time. The competition level was kind of overwhelming.

My parents would come to visit and I would talk to them every day. It was tough because you hadn't struggled before and you hadn't been away from home. Everyone had confidence problems going through that. It was quite an adjustment.

But, I remember going to my first big league spring training, seeing some of the players, and realizing that it wasn't really the talent level but more the consistency that separated guys from the Minor League to the Major Leagues. I think that helped me out a lot.

Some of the older players, like Gerald Williams, took me under his wing and made me feel comfortable. He would talk to me in spring training when I was the youngest one. That, and once I got to know more people, made me more comfortable.

The bus trips were the worst! When you were on the bus for twelve hours, it was not fun. I definitely don't miss those.

We didn't really have food except for peanut butter and jelly, and I like peanut butter and jelly, but that got old when you ate it every single day for one hundred and forty-something games.

Roger LaFrancois

Major League Clubs/Minor League
Organizations: BOSTON RED SOX,
ATLANTA BRAVES

Position: CATCHER

Team: PAWTUCKET, RI

League: INTERNATIONAL

Year: 1981

ROGER LAFRANCOIS played one
year in the Major Leagues with Boston in
1982. If plate appearances didn't matter, it could be argued that Roger was
the last player to hit .400 for the Red Sox after going 4-for-10 at the plate
that season. A hitting disciple of Walter Hriniak and Charlie Lau,
LaFrancois has served as a Minor League hitting instructor at every level
in the Chicago White Sox, New York Mets, and San Francisco Giants
organizations for nearly twenty years.

LaFrancois played six seasons in the Minor Leagues from 1978 to 1985.
His memorable Minor League experience occurred while playing Class
AAA ball in the Boston Red Sox organization.

It was the longest game in baseball history. The game began on
April 18, 1981 and was completed on June 23, 1981 at Paw-
tucket's McCoy Stadium between the visiting Rochester Red
Wings and the home Pawtucket Red Sox.

It was suspended over eight hours later with the scored tied
2–2 after thirty-two innings. I came into the game to catch for
Rich Gedman after he was pinch-hit and pinch-run for.

I thought that it would only be for a few innings, and I ended
up catching twenty-four innings. From the ninth inning on,
neither team scored a run through the twenty-first inning. Then,
in the top of the twenty-first, Rochester scored a run. But, in the
bottom of the inning, we tied it up.

A lot of notables played in that game, like Cal Ripken, Jr., Wade Boggs, Bobby Ojeda, Bruce Hurst, Marty Barrett, and Gedman just to name a few.

During that time, there was a Major League Baseball strike. When the game resumed, we were the story. I remember that there was a big media crowd from all over the country in Pawtucket. I think that helped to get the Pawtucket Red Sox off the ground. They weren't doing all that well at the time, but were suddenly rejuvenated by all of the press.

I was 2-for-8 and walked a couple of times. It was quite ironic, because I had about 10 at-bats in that game and in the entire 1982 season with Boston, I only had 10 at-bats. The game was tough for some guys, too. There was one player on the team who went 0-for-11 with around seven strikeouts. Another one of my teammates, who got home at about 5:30 in the morning, wasn't allowed into his house by his wife because she didn't believe that game lasted until 4:09 A.M. before it was suspended. She thought that he was out gallivanting around. He had to go back to the ballpark to sleep in the clubhouse.

Finally, when the game resumed about two months later, Dave Koza hit a bloop single to right field in the bottom of the thirty-third inning to score Barrett and end the game. The next morning, Dave was on *Good Morning America.*

We only played one inning in the second part of the game and then played our regularly scheduled game right after that. I actually hit a home run in the second game, but by then, nobody was there to see it. Once the first game ended, all of the media left.

I'll never forget how the first part of the game was played on a cold and rainy night. The wind was blowing in and it was really just miserable. But, it's something that I will never forget and I feel very fortunate to have been a part of it.

Adam Piatt

Major League Clubs/Minor League Organizations:
TAMPA BAY DEVIL RAYS, OAKLAND ATHLETICS,
CLEVELAND INDIANS
Position: OUTFIELDER
Team: MEDFORD, OR
League: NORTHWEST
Year: 1997

ADAM PIATT broke into the Major Leagues with the Oakland A's in 2000 and batted .299 in 60 games during his rookie season. As a top prospect on his way to the big leagues, he won the Texas League Triple Crown in 1999 with a .345 batting average, 39 home runs, and 135 RBI while playing for Double-A Midland.

Piatt played parts of six seasons in the Minor Leagues from 1997 to 2002. His memorable Minor League experience occurred while playing Class A ball in the Oakland Athletics organization.

I have always been considered a team prankster.

It was my first year in pro ball after playing at Mississippi State, and I had a teammate that I knew who played at Auburn. There was an early and late bus going to the ballpark that day, and my teammate took the early bus to the field.

After the bus left, I went to the hotel front desk and pretended to be my teammate who just left for the field. Because the attendant did not know either one of us, I was able to convince the attendant that I was my teammate and got a key to his room.

I immediately went into his room, laid a bath towel on the floor, and defecated on it. I wrapped up the towel, placed it on top of the heater, turned the heater on high, and left for the ballpark on the late bus.

When we got back to the hotel after the game, everyone except "the victim" knew what I did.

As soon as we got on the elevator, you could notice a really bad smell. But by the time we got to the floor of his room, the smell was just horrible.

Jason Phillips

Major League Clubs/Minor League Organizations: NEW YORK METS

Position: FIRST BASE, CATCHER

Team: COLUMBIA, SC

League: SOUTH ATLANTIC

Year: 1999

JASON PHILLIPS became an everyday player for the New York Mets in 2003 after three straight seasons in the Minor Leagues of posting a .300 batting average. A candidate for the National League Rookie of the Year, he batted .298 with 11 home runs and 58 RBI in 119 games in his first full campaign with the Mets.

Phillips played parts of five seasons in the Minor Leagues from 1997 to 2001. His memorable Minor League experience occurred while playing Class A ball in the New York Mets organization.

I had an instance with an umpire in the minors when I was in the South Atlantic League.

The umpire is in the Major Leagues now. He doesn't know this, but we were getting killed by 10 runs or something in the seventh inning, and there was a play at the plate.

The guy was out but he called him safe.

So, I went out to tell our pitcher to throw the next pitch right at his mask. It was a fastball that I played off like it was going to be a split-finger in the dirt. I went down to block the pitch in the dirt and the ball smoked him right in the mask.

I never thought that I would see him again and shoot, six or seven years later, he's in the big leagues, too. The ball hit him so squarely in the mask that it just dropped straight down behind me and the runners didn't even advance.

I did it because it was in the heat of the moment, but looking back, I should not have done that. The guy was okay but he is still brutal, too.

Now, with my brother in the Minor Leagues, I tell him what to avoid, what to go for, and who to sit next to. It's good because all the things he calls about and says, "Man, this is brutal," I tell him that I have been there and beyond, so don't worry about it.

Ryan Bradley

Major League Clubs/Minor League Organizations:
NEW YORK YANKEES, COLORADO ROCKIES
Position: PITCHER
Team: ONEONTA, NY
League: NEW YORK-PENN
Year: 1997

RYAN BRADLEY was a first-round pick of the New York Yankees in 1997 out of Arizona State University. In 1998, he reached the big leagues at twenty-two years old and won two of the 125 record-setting victories for the World Champion Yankees. That season, Bradley accomplished the incredibly rare feat of starting his season with Class A Tampa and finishing his season with the big league club.

Bradley played parts of six seasons in the Minor Leagues from 1997 to 2002. His memorable Minor League experience occurred while playing Class A ball in the New York Yankees organization.

I was in Oneonta, New York, after signing with the New York Yankees.

It was my second day there and I was staying in this little hotel that looked like a cabin. After the game, I went out to get something to eat and came back at around 1 A.M.

At the hotel, the guy behind the counter would not let me in because he said it was too late. He just wouldn't let me in. I was outside, carrying my two bags, yelling at this guy to open the door. He finally let me in.

When I got into my room, there was no telephone. So, I went back to the front desk to tell the guy that there was no telephone. He told me that they didn't have telephones there and that I could use the pay phone. But, because the pay phone was outside and the door was locked, he said that he would not let me back in. It was ridiculous.

We were about a mile and a half from the ballpark, up a hill and across some railroad tracks. There was no way that I was walking to the park everyday.

So, the next morning, a teammate and I walked four miles along the highway to a Kmart to buy skateboards. We bought the skateboards, took our shirts off, got on the highway, and skateboarded back.

On the way, our manager, Tom Arnold, happened to pass us and pulled over. He asked us, "What the hell are you two doing right now?" I said, "Hey Coach, what's up?" He quickly responded, "First of all, I'm your manager. Second of all, what are you doing on a skateboard?"

I told him that I needed transportation.

About two or three days later, the Yankees brass came to town. It was Hall of Fame weekend, and so Yankees owner George Steinbrenner and Vice President Mark Newman were there.

At the park, I hid my skateboard in the back of my locker. Newman found it, asked me why I had a skateboard, and told me take a cab. When I said no, he told me that I better not get hurt.

For the rest of that summer, I rode my skateboard the mile and a half to the park every single day.

Joe Lisio

Major League Clubs/Minor League
Organizations: NEW YORK YANKEES,
NEW YORK METS, CHICAGO WHITE
SOX, ARIZONA DIAMONDBACKS

Position: PITCHER

Team: NORWICH, CT

League: EASTERN

Year: 1999

JOE LISIO had one pitch change his life forever. Unfortunately, it was not for the better. In 1999, Lisio led the Eastern League in saves with 33 and helped the Norwich Navigators of the New York Yankees organization reach the League Championship Series. Now a New York City police officer, Lisio is a starting pitcher for the NYPD baseball team and travels with the club to play against police departments in Chicago, Los Angeles, Toronto, and Miami at their respective Major League stadiums.

Lisio played eight seasons in the Minor Leagues from 1994 to 2001. His memorable Minor League experience occurred while playing Class AA ball in the New York Yankees organization.

Author's Note: The 1999 Eastern League Championship Series between the Norwich Navigators of the New York Yankees organization and the Harrisburg Senators of the Montreal Expos organization had the most dramatic ending in Minor League baseball history. In Game 5 of a best-of-five series, Harrisburg rallied to score five runs in the bottom of the ninth inning to win 12–11 and capture an unprecedented fourth consecutive Eastern League title. The game ended on a grand slam hit by Milton Bradley, who connected on a 3–2 fastball with two outs against league saves leader Joe Lisio.

As usual, I started to prepare for the ninth inning to close out my game.

Now, this situation was a little different. It was like Game 5 of the World Series for me. I was getting a little nervous and my heart was starting to beat a little bit in the bullpen.

In the ninth inning, my manager Lee Mazzilli called on Oswaldo Mairena to come in. When he went in, he threw about twelve straight balls. Now, I started really throwing the ball hard in the bullpen because I knew that I was going to go in soon.

Mazzilli came out and summoned me to the mound. I did my usual jog to the grass and walked to the mound. I took the ball from Mazzilli and he told me, "Eye of the Tiger."

I got the first guy to pop out to shortstop. The next guy was Brian Schneider. Brian Schneider struck out on a split-finger in the dirt. Here I was with two outs, bases loaded and I hadn't given up a run yet. I was one out away from victory.

The next batter was Jason Camilli, and on a 2–2 count, he hit a ground ball to my third baseman Donny Leon. Donny dove for the ball and hurt himself on the play. He couldn't come up and make a throw. I said, "Oh, man!" I had such a great feeling that he was going to come up, throw to first, and that we were going to win.

Now, I had to face Milton Bradley with the bases loaded and the game 11–8. I fell behind Bradley 2–0. I was trying to over-throw and throw the fastball by him because he struck out a few times that day.

At 2–0, I came back with a fastball and got 2–1. I came back with another fastball and got 2–2. I then threw a split-finger but he didn't go for it. It was now 3–2 with the bases loaded. I thought that the pitch at 2–2 was a strike. It was pretty close.

With the fans going nuts and everything going crazy, my mind was just trying to strike out the guy and zone everybody out. I remember that it was loud there. The next pitch, I threw a fastball outside that went inside and he hit it on a line drive.

I saw my right fielder Chip Glass look up, and I thought it was going to be a line drive toward him. But, it hit the top of the double-deck wall. It was a rocket that went out so fast. As he hit the home run, I thought, "Oh, shit."

When I let go of the pitch, I knew it was a mistake. Like a typical lefty, he hit the inside pitch. Everyone was throwing him away the whole time, and I just missed my spot.

My heart went down to my stomach because I knew that we just lost the game. I felt bad for all of my teammates because I felt like I let everybody down. I even started to cry in the locker room because it was such a letdown. I was just one out away.

Not to make any excuses, because the guy did hit a shot, but if I came in the ninth inning with nobody on, I would have got the job done and we would have won the game. Mazzilli came up to me in the clubhouse at the end of the game and said that it was his fault.

The next day, I had to read about it in the papers and it was even on ESPN. To this day, five years later, I still think about it. It was the worst experience I ever had in baseball, in life, by far.

Brian Schneider

Major League Clubs/Minor League Organizations:
MONTREAL EXPOS

Position: CATCHER

Team: HARRISBURG, PA

League: EASTERN

Year: 1999

BRIAN SCHNEIDER developed into one of the best defensive catchers in the National League in 2004. In a breakout season, he caught a career best 133 games and committed only two errors, yielding an impressive fielding percentage of .998. In addition, he posted career highs in hits with 112, home runs with 12, and RBI with 49. Schneider led the Major Leagues in throwing out runners attempting to steal a base, nailing 36 of 72 would-be base thieves.

Schneider played parts of seven seasons in the Minor Leagues from 1995 to 2001. His memorable Minor League experience occurred while playing Class AA ball in the Montreal Expos organization.

Author's Note: The 1999 Eastern League Championship Series between the Norwich Navigators of the New York Yankees organization and the Harrisburg Senators of the Montreal Expos organization had the most dramatic ending in Minor League baseball history. In Game 5 of a best-of-five series, Harrisburg rallied to score five runs in the bottom of the ninth inning to win 12–11 and capture an unprecedented fourth consecutive Eastern League title. The game ended on a grand slam hit by Milton Bradley, who connected on a 3–2 fastball with two outs against league saves leader Joe Lisio.

It was a miserable night being that it was raining.

You almost knew that something weird was going to happen that night with the way the weather was and with the fans sticking it out throughout the rain.

We were not that good of a team the whole season, but we made a run in the last month to make the playoffs. We got so far and knew that we wanted to win the championship, but just to be in that position was a great accomplishment for us.

As the game went on, it went back and forth where they would score a couple of runs and we would score a couple of runs. Norwich made a last push in the ninth and were up four runs going into the bottom of the ninth. Everyone knew that we could do it, but deep down it was hard to believe.

We got a few guys on after a couple of walks. I had a big at-bat and didn't come through. You want to do so much for the team and get that big hit but it just didn't happen for me. After the out, I remember walking back to the dugout with my head down and feeling real disappointed. I felt terrible going into the dugout knowing that could be my last at-bat that year.

But then there was the play where the ball was hit to Donny Leon. He dove for it and hurt his shoulder. He couldn't get up and make a play. A run scored, kept the bases loaded, and Milton came up.

Milton had come through for us so much during the season. I remember earlier in that inning, before we made the rally, I went into the clubhouse and saw Milton sitting in a chair in front of his locker with his head down.

He was mad because we gave up those runs. He wanted to win so bad after getting that far. I sat down and talked to Milton, telling him that anything could happen and that he had to get out there because we needed him.

When he came up to bat, I couldn't take it. The count went to 3–2. Then, right when that ball hit the bat, I immediately did a dead sprint to home plate while watching the ball. Right after he hit it, he started to undo both batting gloves and walking a little bit. Everyone was yelling, "Run!" But I guess he knew it was out.

When the first person touched home plate, I was there and jumped into his arms. It was the most unbelievable feeling. As we were waiting for Milton to come around third base, I remember looking out at the field to see the scoreboard and seeing guys from Norwich down on one knee, laying on their back or just standing there in disbelief.

For us to do that, in the pouring rain and with all the fans supporting us, was just unbelievable.

I still have my ring. I don't really ever wear it, but every now and then I will put it on just to remember. I know they still talk about it in Harrisburg. I still talk about it with guys like Nick Johnson, Brad Wilkerson, and Tony Armas, Jr.

I remember being surprised that Joe Lisio didn't start the ninth inning. Seeing him warming up leading up to that inning, we didn't understand what was going on. For him not to start it, I guess Lee Mazzilli had something else planned.

But I remember that he gave up an opposite-field grand slam to Jon Tucker there earlier in the season.

It was Harrisburg's fourth straight championship. After the game, the mayor was saying that of all the stories you will ever hear, this by far will do them in. You will always remember the Milton Bradley home run to win the series.

As far as learning a lesson from baseball, I think that if anyone can ever get anything out of this story, it's that it is never over until the last out is made. We were down four runs in the bottom of the ninth inning. So much stuff can happen with two outs.

They make T-shirts about that. You're down three runs, you're up to bat, the bases are loaded, it's a 3–2 count in Game

5 in the ninth inning, it's raining out, the best closer in the league is on the mound and you hit a home run.

You can't script that at eight or nine years old in the backyard playing Wiffle Ball. I know I have never seen or been involved in a game that ended any better than that.

Aaron Miles

Major League Clubs/Minor League Organizations:
HOUSTON ASTROS, CHICAGO WHITE SOX,
COLORADO ROCKIES
Position: CATCHER
Team: KISSIMMEE, FL
League: FLORIDA STATE
Year: 2000

AARON MILES battled for nine years in the Minor Leagues before he finally got his chance in the big leagues in 2003 with the Chicago White Sox. Following that season, he was traded to the Colorado Rockies for shortstop Juan Uribe and batted .293 with six home runs and 47 RBI in his rookie year. In 861 career Minor League games, Miles hit .289 with 43 homers, 380 RBI, and 135 stolen bases.

Miles played parts of ten seasons in the Minor Leagues from 1995 to 2004. His memorable Minor League experience occurred while playing Class A ball in the Houston Astros organization.

I was in Kissimmee with the Astros in spring training in 2000. I was coming back to my hotel room when I saw that my door was open. Six of my teammates, who were in the next room over, were being held hostage. I went into my room and ended up being held hostage too for about forty minutes.

I ended up wrestling with the guy for his gun. I was kind of on top of him and we were both holding the gun. The cops came in and wound up having to shoot the guy.

They came in and shot the guy six times.

Cal Ripken, Jr.

Major League Clubs/Minor League Organizations:
BALTIMORE ORIOLES

Position: SHORTSTOP, THIRD BASE

Team: BLUEFIELD, WV

League: APPALACHIAN

Year: 1978

RIPKEN played parts of four seasons in the Minor Leagues from 1978 to 1981. His memorable Minor League experience occurred while playing Class A ball in the Baltimore Orioles organization.

The Minor Leagues were a big awakening as soon as you were drafted.

Say you were one of the better players and it was obvious that you were one of the stars of the team in high school. Then, all of a sudden, all of the stars from high school, and college, go through the draft and a little mini-camp. You would look around and say, "Man, I don't know if I am going to make it."

In one of my first experiences, there was a shortstop named Bob Bonner. He was drafted out of Texas A&M in a lower round than I was, which was maybe the third or fourth round while I was in the second round.

I was taking ground balls next to him. He was five years older than I was and he had a great arm. I thought to myself, "I am never going to play." They sent him to Double-A right away, and so he was out of our rookie ball team.

We all had the dream, but I don't think that any of us thought that we were going to make it. There was nothing that separated us in the first couple of years in the minors. I started getting hits in the second half of Miami, and things started to fall into place. I started to look around, relatively speaking, and thought that

I had a chance. I got called up to Double-A at the end of that year, but it wasn't until I had a breakout year in Double-A when I said that I was going to make it.

I grew up with my Dad managing in the Minor Leagues.

I was in the small towns, and so I saw the quaintness and beauty of being around the Minor Leagues. I think that sort of training helped me. Coming from high school, I thought it was glamorous.

We didn't draw a lot of people, but some of the ballparks had a few people in them. They all screamed and you could hear everything they said. The fewer people in the stands, the more clearly you could hear them ragging on you. But just that environment, in a professional way, with crowds, funny promotions, and being in a ballpark that had seats, I thought it was glamorous.

I think that I had an advantage in some ways because there was an adjustment period for people coming into pro ball. That adjustment period a lot of times was being homesick. Going away for the first time and being on your own for the first time. You were problem solving and not really knowing what to expect.

There was an adjustment that you had to make so that it wouldn't negatively affect your performance. The more that you worried about some of those other things, like being homesick, missing your parents and wishing that you home in a secure environment, the more that would take away from your game.

Growing up around Minor League baseball, I had a really good idea of what to expect. We had gone to many different towns. We packed up the car and drove to where Dad was. And even though I wasn't on my own back then, I went to the ballpark with Dad and hung around the ballpark. I was comfortable in those surroundings more so than some of my teammates.

Now, I think being involved in Minor League baseball (in Aberdeen, Maryland) has put me back in touch with some of my early beginnings, like the excitement of being drafted and going through the system.

I can see an honest excitement on all of the players. I am glad that I am associated with an entry-level group. This is their first look into pro ball. There is a genuine excitement and hope that you can really see in the Minor Leagues.

I love watching the kids with that dream, hope, and determination. It's really what happens in the first few years that will give you some hope to think you can make it, or you are going to have to find another job.

Marcus Thames

Major League Clubs/Minor League Organizations:
NEW YORK YANKEES, TEXAS RANGERS, DETROIT TIGERS
Position: OUTFIELDER
Team: NORWICH, CT
League: EASTERN
Year: 2001

THAMES played parts of eight seasons in the Minor Leagues from 1997 to 2004. His memorable Minor League experience occurred while playing Class AA ball in the New York Yankees organization.

In 2001, David Justice came down to Norwich on a rehab.

I remember how he worked hard every day. He never acted like he was way up above us, even though he was, and just seemed like a normal guy. He told us stories about how you wanted to be up in the big leagues, and showed us his World Series ring that he won with the Yankees.

He said to me, "The way the ball jumps off your bat, Marcus, you will definitely be a Major League Baseball player."

When he told me that, a guy who played the game and had a lot of success in it, it really pumped me up. I always really appreciated that.

Then, we had an off-day and there was a Monday afternoon game at Yankee Stadium. I told him that I wanted to go to the game, and he said that he would leave me tickets. He left me four tickets, and I went down with a friend of mine.

It was the first time I had ever walked into Yankee Stadium. I immediately noticed all of the tradition. Coming up in the Yankees organization, I obviously really wanted to get there. But, it was by going to a game first before I played there.

I walked out to Monument Park and took pictures and stuff. I said to myself, "Hopefully one day I can play out here."

Mike Piazza

Major League Clubs/Minor League Organizations:
NEW YORK METS, LOS ANGELES DODGERS,
FLORIDA MARLINS

Position: CATCHER

Team: BAKERSFIELD, CA

League: CALIFORNIA

Year: 1991

PIAZZA played parts of four seasons in the Minor Leagues from 1989 to 1992. His memorable Minor League experience occurred while playing Class A ball in the Los Angeles Dodgers organization.

After my first year, I was fumbling around a bit and didn't really develop. I was getting older and got so frustrated one year that I wanted to quit. I didn't feel like I was getting any better and just wasn't having any fun, either.

But when I wanted to quit, I soon figured out that I only had one time in my life to do this. I decided that I was going to go back, have fun, enjoy myself, not put pressure on myself, play hard, work hard, and give it one last shot.

I'm glad I was able to do that. But that was part of the whole maturation process. You mature and become a man through that experience.

I was in the Cal League and some guy behind the plate was on me so bad. He was calling me "Pizza" and I was really struggling. He was ripping me like I have never been ripped before. There were like twenty people in the stands and you could hear every single word.

I wanted to kill this guy but then it got to the point where it was actually funny. I'll never forget that. After I got out of the game, I was so frustrated, so ticked off, and struggling so bad that I took a bat, signed it, and gave this guy the bat. He was like, "Holy smoke," and completely stunned.

There was a pitcher in the stands that I played with who just couldn't believe it. He told me that the guy was all over me the whole game.

Well, it got to the point where I was taking myself too seriously. I realized that I should relax and just have fun.

Pete Walker

Major League Clubs/Minor League Organizations:
NEW YORK METS, SAN DIEGO PADRES,
BOSTON RED SOX, COLORADO ROCKIES,
TORONTO BLUE JAYS
Position: PITCHER
Team: ST. LUCIE, FL
League: FLORIDA STATE
Year: 1991

WALKER spent parts of fourteen seasons in the Minor Leagues from 1990 to 2003. His memorable Minor League experience occurred while playing Class A ball in the New York Mets organization.

It was 1991, and Brook Fordyce and I were playing together for the St. Lucie Mets in the Florida State League.

We had an off-day, and Brook and I had gone with a number of other teammates down to West Palm Beach to get away from baseball for the day. After we had a great time down there, we were coming back very late at night.

It was about 4 A.M., and I think that I can say that now because it was a very long time ago. We were driving back to his place in Jensen Beach, where we both stayed for the summer. It was actually his parents' condo overlooking the Atlantic Ocean.

I was driving along when I noticed something dark ahead in the road. Suddenly, it disappeared about fifty yards away from us, but I didn't think much of it. As we continued to drive, there was a massive thud and the car buckled. I had definitely run over something.

We pulled off to the side of the road, staring at each other in amazement. We were also pretty scared, but both of us got out of the car and walked back. Our minds were racing. As we got closer, we noticed it was a huge creature.

Well, it turned out to be a ten-foot alligator. The alligator was not moving, and we decided not to get too close. However, at one point, I was probably only about five feet away from this thing. This was on a causeway off of I-95, and it was really dark. The only way we could see was from the brake lights of the car.

So, we got back in the car, called the proper authorities and drove away.

Gary Sheffield

Major League Clubs/Minor League Organizations:
MILWAUKEE BREWERS, SAN DIEGO PADRES, FLORIDA MARLINS,
LOS ANGELES DODGERS, ATLANTA BRAVES, NEW YORK YANKEES
Position: OUTFIELD
Team: EL PASO, TX
League: TEXAS
Year: 1988

SHEFFIELD played parts of four seasons in the Minor Leagues from 1986 to 1989. His memorable Minor League experience occurred while playing Class AA ball in the Milwaukee Brewers organization.

When I went up to Double-A in El Paso, and you hit a home run at Diablo Stadium, everyone knew that you had to go along the stands with your hat and collect dollar bills.

You got to keep the money and would use it to pay your rent. It drove you to hit home runs because it helped take care of you. I would get two pairs of boots for free.

One particular time, I hit a home run and forgot to go into the stands because there were two outs when I hit it. I was getting ready to go out when all of a sudden the third out was made. I thought that I had to run on the field. So, I forgot to collect the money.

The next thing I knew, I came out of the stadium and my car was trashed. I went against their tradition.

Mike Lowell

Major League Clubs/Minor League Organizations:
NEW YORK YANKEES, FLORIDA MARLINS
Position: THIRD BASE
Team: ONEONTA, NY
League: NEW YORK-PENN
Year: 1995

LOWELL played parts of five seasons in the Minor Leagues from 1995 to 1999. His memorable Minor League experience occurred while playing Class A ball in the New York Yankees organization.

One of the things that I guess depicts Minor League life was when I was in the New York-Penn League.

I'm not positive of the city, but I think that it was in Auburn, New York. I was with Oneonta, and our hotel was right across the street from a maximum-security prison.

The only place to eat that was open after the game was a gas station on the corner. Because it was A ball and we didn't have any food after the game, we walked to the gas station.

It was on the corner, but across the street on the corner, so it was next to the prison. We went into this place, grabbed a sandwich that was probably in the freezer for four or five days, some chips, and some soda.

We walked out and headed back to the hotel. Then, the security guards from the watchtower of the prison shined the escape lights on us. They wanted to make sure that we weren't anyone trying to get out of the prison.

That was pretty scary. They had rifles and would be looking down watching us. We had to go through that for about three days, and actually got used to it.

Doug Mientkiewicz

Major League Clubs/Minor League Organizations:
MINNESOTA TWINS, BOSTON RED SOX
Position: FIRST BASE
Team: SALT LAKE CITY, UT
League: PACIFIC COAST
Year: 2000

MIENTKIEWICZ played parts of five seasons in the Minor Leagues from 1995 to 2000. His memorable Minor League experience occurred while playing Class AAA ball in the Minnesota Twins organization.

When I was in Triple-A, Phil Roof was my manager in Salt Lake City.

Phil was also a motorcycle rider, and after he won his umpteenth million game in Triple-A, they had a motorcycle out there for him. Well, he tried to ride it from first base, around home plate, and to third base. When he got to home, and it had been raining, he started slipping. He peeled out, slid, and his hand went back on the gas.

They had just sodded the whole infield, and here was this motorcycle spinning grass with chunks of sod flying all over the place.

He broke the motorcycle and ruined our field for three weeks.

Carlos Delgado

Major League Clubs/Minor League Organizations:
TORONTO BLUE JAYS

Position: FIRST BASE

Team: SYRACUSE, NY

League: INTERNATIONAL

Year: 1994

DELGADO played parts of seven seasons in the Minor Leagues from 1989 to 1995. His memorable Minor League experience occurred while playing Class AAA ball in the Toronto Blue Jays organization.

When I was in Triple-A with Syracuse in 1994, that was the year of the strike.

All of the teams were loaded. They sent all of the young guys down from the big leagues to Triple-A to get some playing time. They knew that they were going to strike.

I remember playing Richmond in the Championship and it was a big deal because there was no baseball in the big leagues. It was even on ESPN. Those games might have been the most important games going on in professional baseball in the States.

I thought it was pretty cool because I was in Triple-A and those games were the hot item on TV.

John Franco

Major League Clubs/Minor League Organizations:
LOS ANGELES DODGERS, CINCINNATI REDS, NEW YORK METS

Position: PITCHER

Team: ALBUQUERQUE, NM

League: PACIFIC COAST

Year: 1983

FRANCO played parts of four seasons in the Minor Leagues from 1981 to 1984. His memorable Minor League experience occurred while playing Class AAA ball in the Los Angeles organization.

The best thing that happened to me in the minors was when I was traded in May of 1983 from the Dodgers to the Cincinnati Reds. The funny thing about that was we were in Albuquerque, New Mexico, and our manager was an ex-catcher named Del Crandall.

On that particular day, the guy that was traded with me, Brett Wise, and I were sitting in the bullpen. It was a hot day and we had our hats off taking in the sun. Del was a like real military guy and took no shit. After the game, the pitching coach, Brent Strom, came up and said that Del wanted to see us in his office.

We thought, "Oh shit, he caught us taking in the sun." We went in and he said, "I'm not going to beat around the bush boys, you've been traded to Cincinnati. Good luck and take it easy." That was it.

What was great about that trade was I went to Indianapolis that year and became a starter. I kind of struggled in the sixth and seventh innings, and so in the last month of that season, they moved me to the bullpen. From there, I just took off. The following spring, I went to spring training and really mastered a change-up that I developed with the Dodgers.

Two weeks into that Minor League season, I was called up to the Major Leagues.

Edgardo Alfonzo

Major League Clubs/Minor League Organizations:
NEW YORK METS, SAN FRANCISCO GIANTS

Position: THIRD BASE

Team: ST. LUCIE, FL

League: GULF COAST

Year: 1991

ALFONZO played four seasons in the Minor Leagues from 1991 to 1994. His memorable Minor League experience occurred while playing Class A ball in the New York Mets organization.

I remember in order to save money while in the instructional league, we would eat grapefruits off of the trees at our complex in Florida for breakfast everyday.

Three guys would live together, and we lived across from where the coaches lived. But, because the coaches had vans, we would have to get up everyday at 5 A.M. to catch a ride with them to get to the field.

There were a lot of good and bad things that happened in the Minor Leagues. But for all of the sacrificing we did then, I see the results now as a big league player.

Doug Glanville

Major League Clubs/Minor League Organizations:
PHILADELPHIA PHILLIES, CHICAGO CUBS,
TEXAS RANGERS

Position: OUTFIELDER

Team: ORLANDO

League: SOUTHERN

Year: 1994

GLANVILLE played six seasons in the Minor Leagues from 1991 to 1996.
His memorable Minor League experience occurred while playing Class AA
ball in the Chicago Cubs organization.

I had a lot of fun in the Minor Leagues. One year I played
against Michael Jordan, which was the year he played with
Birmingham and I was with Orlando. We would tape the games.
My brother would come with a camcorder.

Then, after the season in the Arizona Fall League, we actually played pick-up basketball together. That was probably not
completely legal at the time. A bunch of guys got together, like
twenty or twenty-five guys, and played.

He played hard, but I'm not going to say that he played like
he would in the NBA Championship. He played hard enough
that he wasn't happy when we ended up winning.

To watch him on the court was amazing. He was at such
another level. How he jumped and just did everything. It was
unbelievable.

Derek Lowe

Major League Clubs/Minor League Organizations:
SEATTLE MARINERS, BOSTON RED SOX

Position: PITCHER

Team: JACKSONVILLE, FL

League: SOUTHERN

Year: 1994

LOWE played parts of seven seasons in the Minor Leagues from 1991 to 1997. His memorable Minor League experience occurred while playing Class AA ball in the Seattle Mariners organization.

In the Minor Leagues, none of us had any money.

The things you would do for money. I remember one time in Jacksonville, it was pouring rain and the dugouts filled up with water and so much other crap. There was a guy on the team that said to us, "How much would it take for me to drink a cup full of this crap?"

Guys started throwing in like fifty bucks and it turned out to be $500 to $1,000. So, he filled up a Powerade cup and drank it.

That was the crazy stuff that you would do just for money. One, to pass the time, and two, a thousand dollars back then, when you are making $1,500 a month, was huge.

Luis Sojo

Major League Clubs/Minor League Organizations:
NEW YORK YANKEES, TORONTO BLUE JAYS,
CALIFORNIA ANGELS, SEATTLE MARINERS,
PITTSBURGH PIRATES
Position: INFIELDER/THIRD BASE COACH
Team: MYRTLE BEACH, SC
League: SOUTH ATLANTIC
Year: 1987

SOJO played parts of eight seasons in the Minor League from 1987 to 1995. His memorable Minor League experience occurred while playing Class A ball in the Toronto Blue Jays organization.

In Myrtle Beach, our clubhouse was a trailer.

Our pitching coach was Bill Monbouquette and his car was always parked over near the trailer. There was an open field by the clubhouse where some older guys would hit golf balls. They knew that we played for the Myrtle Beach Blue Jays, and one day they let us have a couple of swings.

Well, one of my teammates asked if he could hit one. He grabbed the club, took a huge baseball swing, and hit a line drive that went straight through the back door of our pitching coach's car.

My goodness, it wasn't a dent, it was a huge hole. He smoked that ball. It just went right through the door. I don't remember what kind of car it was, but I remember it was a nice dark brown car.

We got called into a meeting that day with Bill and he said that if he ever found the people who did that, he would kill them. During the meeting, we just sat there and didn't look at one another.

I don't think Bill ever found out who it was.

Chris Woodward

Major League Clubs/Minor League Organizations:
TORONTO BLUE JAYS
Position: SHORTSTOP
Team: HAGERSTOWN, MD
League: SOUTH ATLANTIC
Year: 1996

WOODWARD played parts of eight seasons in the Minor Leagues from
1995 to 2001. His memorable Minor League experience occurred while
playing Class A ball in the Toronto Blue Jays organization.

I was coming out of junior college in 1995, and going to play
pro ball in Medicine Hat, Alberta.

The first couple of months, I struggled pretty bad. The season was only about three months long. I was hitting just over
.200 and thinking to myself, "What's going on?"

We were playing the number-one team at the time, which
was Billings, Montana. They had this 6–6 closer throwing about
95 miles per hour. Every time that we played them, he came in
and blew us away. It was a big game for us because we were
neck and neck with them for the lead and only about a game out.

Sure enough, I came up in the bottom of the ninth with two
outs and the tying run at third base. The closer was in, and
before I got up, the manager pulled me aside for some reason.
He told me that I was going to win the game for us. I thought
to myself, "Wow, that's kind of cool. No one has ever done that
to me during a game before."

I got up to bat, and right away, fell behind 0–2. Somehow, I
fouled away some tough pitches and on one particular slider, I
just got a piece of it to stay alive. I worked the count to 3-and-
2 with a man on third and two outs. He threw me a fastball and

I hit it pretty good to left center. I went on a dead sprint because I didn't know if it was going to go out or not.

By the time I got to second base, I saw everyone running off the field. I had never hit a home run in pro ball before. I immediately had an adrenaline rush because I just won the game. There were maybe fifteen people in the stands. It was unbelievable. I still have never experienced anything like that again.

When I got to home, my manager just gave me a little wink. My teammates were going nuts and they went and got the ball for me.

My mom still has the ball at home in a little case.

Walt Hriniak

Major League Clubs/Minor League Organizations:
MILWAUKEE BRAVES, ATLANTA BRAVES, SAN DIEGO PADRES
Position: CATCHER/HITTING COACH
Team: JAMESTOWN, NY
League: NEW YORK-PENN
Year: 1972

HRINIAK played eleven seasons in the Minor Leagues from 1961 to 1971 and began coaching in 1972. His memorable Minor League experience occurred while coaching Class A ball in the Montreal Expos organization.

In my first year managing in 1972 in Jamestown, New York, I had thirty-six players and didn't have a coach.

I was all by myself and had three workouts a day at 10 o'clock in the morning, two o'clock in the afternoon, and then regular practice at five o'clock. We dragged the field ourselves; we didn't have a grounds crew. The batting screen that I had was a wheelbarrow. I would put a wheelbarrow in front of the pitcher's mound. That was my batting screen.

The Minor Leagues are a lot different than the big leagues. In a lot of ways, the players are a lot closer, and there isn't as much jealousy. It's a lot tighter. While it's not where you wanted to be, as you eventually want to get to the big leagues, the Minor Leagues were a great experience.

Sandy Alomar, Jr.

Major League Clubs/Minor League Organizations:
CLEVELAND INDIANS, CHICAGO WHITE SOX,
COLORADO ROCKIES, SAN DIEGO PADRES

Position: CATCHER

Team: RENO, NV

League: CALIFORNIA

Year: 1984

ALOMAR played parts of six seasons in the Minor Leagues from 1984 to 1989. His memorable Minor League experience occurred while playing Class A ball in the San Diego Padres organization.

Before they sent me to rookie ball in Spokane, they sent me to long-A ball in Reno, Nevada.

Reno was the coldest place that I have played in April. In fact, I didn't even play there. I was just catching bullpens. I was a skinny guy from Puerto Rico, so I wasn't used to the cold weather. It was freezing in April, and I only had one glove. It was an old McGregor glove that was so old it had no padding.

Mitch Williams was there, and I would have to warm him up in the bullpen. He was hard to catch because he was real wild. The pocket of the glove was so thin that I would have to put newspaper inside of it to protect my hand.

You were hungry all the time, but you had to skip a few meals because you didn't have enough money to eat. You would have to pay your clubhouse dues, your rent, and stuff like that. So, we used to buy a quarter of a gallon of milk with a Milky Way or Snickers bar and eat it for lunch because we didn't have enough money for a good meal.

I was making maybe $10 a day in meal money and a salary of about $800 a month in A ball. But just your rent alone was like $500 a month. If you lived by yourself, you would have to sleep on the floor because you could not afford anything else. It was a struggle.

I was eighteen years old when I was first living on my own in the Minor Leagues. I was already a skinny kid to begin with when I signed. I weighed about 175 pounds and was 6'2" or so. I couldn't put on weight because of the way we were eating.

After the game, there would be some food in the locker room but guys were so hungry that, if you got there late, the food was gone. It was stuff like small sandwiches, potato chips, and chocolate bars.

I would try to sacrifice my meals during the week so I could have a good meal on the weekends.

Paul Konerko

Major League Clubs/Minor League Organizations:
LOS ANGELES DODGERS, CHICAGO WHITE SOX
Position: FIRST BASE
Team: SAN BERNARDINO, CA
League: CALIFORNIA
Year: 1995

KONERKO played parts of five seasons in the Minor Leagues from 1994 to 1998. His memorable Minor League experience occurred while playing Class A ball in the Los Angeles Dodgers organization.

The ballpark in San Bernardino was as bad as it gets. It was an old, run-down stadium in a bad area.

I remember one night coming back from a commuter trip and seeing three or four kids breaking into the clubhouse. It was about 12 midnight, and we caught them in the act. These kids were scattering from the clubhouse with equipment and stuff.

Obviously, the cops were called but the kids were long gone.

Gabe Kapler

Major League Clubs/Minor League Organizations:
DETROIT TIGERS, TEXAS RANGERS,
BOSTON RED SOX

Position: OUTFIELDER

Team: LAKELAND, FL

League: FLORIDA STATE

Year: 1997

KAPLER played parts of eight seasons in the Minor Leagues from 1995 to 2003. His memorable Minor League experience occurred while playing Class A ball in the Detroit Tigers organization.

My favorite baseball story, which is somewhat graphic, was in A ball in the Florida State League.

One of my teammates, who was also my roommate, and I were in our hotel room. I was in the bathroom and he had to go really bad. He was banging on the door and I told him that he had to wait. Then, I heard the door slam a couple of times outside of the room.

Well, when I came out of the bathroom, I saw that he tried to defecate in the trash can but completely missed. He had defecated all over the hotel room floor!

He took a whole bunch of white towels and was trying to clean it up. I'm sure you could imagine what type of mess it was. He almost threw up trying to do it.

It was the very worst Minor League experience ever. That's the first one that always pops up in my head when I talk about my Minor League experiences.

It doesn't really have anything to do with being on the field, but I think it tells you a little bit about how Minor League baseball was.

Ellis Burks

Major League Clubs/Minor League Organizations:
BOSTON RED SOX, CHICAGO WHITE SOX,
COLORADO ROCKIES, SAN FRANCISCO GIANTS,
CLEVELAND INDIANS
Position: CENTER FIELD
Team: NEW BRITAIN, CT
League: EASTERN
Year: 1985

BURKS played parts of five seasons in the Minor Leagues from 1983 to 1987. His memorable Minor League experience occurred while playing Class A ball in the Boston Red Sox organization.

The worst ballpark that I played in during the Minor Leagues was Wahconah Park in Pittsfield, Massachusetts.

The sun set in center field, and the umpire had to call time and stop the game. We would have to sit there for forty to forty-five minutes until the sun went down.

Then, they would bring the pitcher back out on the mound and start playing again.

John Flaherty

Major League Clubs/Minor League Organizations:
NEW YORK YANKEES, TAMPA BAY DEVIL RAYS,
BOSTON RED SOX, DETROIT TIGERS

Position: CATCHER

Team: PAWTUCKET, RI

League: INTERNATIONAL

Year: 1993

FLAHERTY played parts of seven seasons in the Minor Leagues from 1988 to 1994. His memorable Minor League experience occurred while playing Class AAA ball in the Boston Red Sox organization.

B ack then, I remember the San Diego Chicken was big. He did a couple of games that I was involved in, and he always had a lot of back-and-forth going on with the catcher.

I was with the Red Sox playing the Phillies in Scranton. He had a Pete Rose skit, when he came around third and barreled over the catcher. Then, he would redo it backward in slow motion.

The funniest part about it was as he was walking me through the whole thing and telling me what to do, I was thinking to myself, "The Chicken is telling me what to do right now."

Wade Boggs

Major League Clubs/Minor League Organizations:
BOSTON RED SOX, NEW YORK YANKEES,
TAMPA BAY DEVIL RAYS

Position: THIRD BASE

Team: ELMIRA, NY

League: NEW YORK-PENN

Year: 1976

BOGGS played six seasons in the Minor Leagues from 1976 to 1981. His memorable Minor League experience occurred while playing Class A ball in the Boston Red Sox organization.

My first year in pro ball was in Elmira, New York. That really molded me. I got my first taste of being away from home. We won it that year and went 50–20. Anytime you go 50–20, I think it speaks volumes for the kind of team that you had. I got a championship ring and still have it. It was the only thing that I had won to that point because I had never been on a winning team as a youth baseball player.

Our manager, Dick Berardino, did a phenomenal job of policing forty-two players and a twenty-five-man clubhouse. That was something you didn't see every day. I had just come out of high school and we had forty-two players from everywhere, like Puerto Rico, the Dominican Republic, college, high school, and all around the United States.

I can remember everything like it was yesterday. I flew into the airport on a Sunday afternoon in June and everything was closed. The players were put up at a women's college in Elmira, but there was nobody around. I couldn't find Dick and I didn't have anyone's phone number. I finally wound up going to a motel and spent the night there.

On the way to the motel, I saw a guy named John Tagliarino from Tampa. He was three years ahead of me in youth baseball and was back in Elmira because of some arm problems. He recognized me and picked me up for our workout at 10 A.M. the next morning. He showed me the ropes and took me around.

Everything was just a culture shock. Buying your own food and doing your own laundry made you grow up fast. My girlfriend at the time, who is now my wife and has been for twenty-seven years, came up to visit me. I proposed to her in late July while I was in Elmira and then we came home and got married in December.

It was a whirlwind year.

Index

STATISTICAL RESEARCH COURTESY

The Baseball Cube
Baseball Almanac
Baseball Reference